A PROCESS MIND

A Timeless Journey of Identifying Problems and Creating Effective Solutions

RICHARDS P. LYON, M.D.

Richards S. P. Lyon

To

Lorrest

Dr. Dick on 5-12-11

Outskirts Press, Inc.
Denver, Colorado

Acknowledgments

Without the encouragement of daughters Kathy, Joan, and Laura, and wife Carol, this story would never have gotten off the ground. Without Cece Morken Gadda, it would never have flown, as she monitored every thought, word, phrase, and comma. Without the heart of Bruce, there would have been no story.

Dedication

This story is dedicated to William Bruce Lyon, who gave his life for his country and bequeathed to his brothers his Joy of Life, which we have tried to channel effectively, so that others may share this precious bounty.

Table of Contents

Preface

I am approaching the midline of the tenth decade of a charmed life, if judged by the quality of lives seen in most of the world. In America, that is not the case, for freedom and opportunity exist to such a degree that charmed lives are common. Most "best sellers" depict the highly successful, as measured in power or wealth, as having overcome a traumatic childhood. I, on the other hand, like so many others, had all of the advantages of a concerned, loving, disciplined home in an upper middle class world. Despite these advantages, I still became successful, but my concept of success had nothing to do with power or wealth. It did require a comfortable living. But above all, it demanded that, whenever possible, *I give something back*.

The story I try to tell is studded with "give-backs," a natural result of a mindset about which little has been written. I didn't recognize what this mindset was until well into my retirement eighties, when my days and nights provided ample time for a life's review. One of my give-backs was diminishing the chance of a fatal pulmonary embolism with surgery or travel. Another was making the weighing of patients routine to prevent fluid balance mistakes, often fatal. A third introduced the catheter to keep congenitally incontinent children dry and thus active, social participants. A fourth altered kidney surgery to make it quicker and less painful. Free time allowed my still fully active mind to keep asking new questions.

And finally, there is the hope that I have told of real life experiences, many humorous, but revealing enough to let those not physicians in on our professional secrets. What a wonderful trip this has been, as the memories preserved by my Process Mind surface to be lived again and again, a practice that resulted from my forays into areas that others had not tread. What did I see or just stumble on, as I took a moment to notice what made me stumble? In so doing, perhaps a hidden truth had surfaced? Then an answer appeared.

It dawned on me that my inability to marshal a Quick Memory was in reality a great blessing. I had considered this a deficit as I watched the "straight A" students easily be accepted into whatever specialty they chose to follow. My admission to medical school had required other qualities than just getting top grades. Today, where sheer numbers of applicants demand that machines replace human judgments, the personal element is often lost. The paradox is that the Process Mind is needed everywhere and more than ever. This type of mind has a peculiar need for mentors, for its never-ending questions must be answered. I hope I can encourage such minds to persevere. Thus, I relate my own Process Mind story as one of doing something every day for someone, while fulfilling the commitment to home and family.

My Process Mind works like this: I must *understand* to remember. This takes more time than is required by the Quick Memory minds. However, it is the *remembering* that makes the difference, allowing me to tell this story today in the hope that I will be effective.

I have come to believe that enthusiasm, call it passion, is a catalyst, unquenchable and indestructible, at times allowing one to accomplish what seems impossible. The Process Mind is ideally suited for this endeavor, for it demands basic truths to be stored and recalled. Possibilities of new concepts and new uses fan out, requiring only solid judgment as to their value and their doable potentials.

Who do I hope will read this story? First will be high school students wondering what is ahead and how their journeys may be influenced by an understanding as to how they learn and remember. Recognition of the Process Mind and its characteristics can make all the difference, as curiosities abound and mentors are sought and recognized. I would wish to be one of them.

Their parents are next in line, especially the new ones, searching for guidance as they direct young lives flowering before them. It is critical that the slower-to-remember Process Minds be recognized and stimulated early on.

I hope medical educators will read here about how one of their own has used his or her Process Mind to contribute solidly, and will recognize the creative potentials lying in such minds, as they not only leave something, but stimulate fellow students to awaken their own processing potentials. Surely, to have both a Quick Memory and a Process Memory acting in concert is a gift with immense potential. It is likely to be the process component that is the driver. At home and in the classroom, a start at uncovering and stimulating the thinking potential of a child, whether naturally a Quick Memorizer or Process Thinker, would be to counter questionable statements with, "Please explain." This would seem to be well within the reach of the concerned parent. Would the modern schoolroom make time for this exploration? Surgeons can relive experiences, perhaps even more poignant than my own, as I expose the workings of our medical minds under trying circumstances.

Retired physicians as a group should, with a little time on their hands, chuckle at events I have described, perhaps unearthing their experiences not thought of for a long time and to be relished in the retelling and hearing. In addition, car lovers should share with me the joys of driving their "Blue Beauties" and vicariously racing at Bondurant Speedway.

Historians must not be left out, for much that is documented here will reveal the characteristics of the part of America I represent, as it chronicles one family's trials and joys in a privileged century of freedom, at times contested, but which in the end is a monument to the America envisioned by our founding fathers almost 250 years ago.

CHAPTER

1.

The Beginning

I was born

I have been reading another success story. It is so wholesome that I wonder if
I would be reading it if the subject were
not already a famous person. Be that as
it may, I will assume that someday, probably long after I am gone, I could be a
famous memory. So why don't I tell my
version as to how I got there, while I can
still be put on the spot with questions.

First, let me make it clear that I was not raised in poverty, was not
mistreated, and have never thrown a punch in anger or as a defense. I
had what many could call an idyllic childhood and yet I made good,
if personal satisfaction with how I have used my days is to be the
judge.

I was born at home in Oakland. Albert Meads, later to become
"Uncle Bert," delivered me at 125 Grand Avenue in a day when
hospital deliveries had become almost the rule. He had been a family
doctor for some years. Then, as specialties began to appear, he went
to the Midwest to train as a urologist with one of the icons of that
time. He returned, accredited by this minimal specialty experience,
yet his family practice habits stayed with him until the day he died.
He loved people. Bringing them into the world was his apex of
achievement.

I come into our world at the end of World War I

As a tiny tot on Grand Avenue I had no understanding that Dad was at death's door. The 1918 flu epidemic had taken him down as he worked in the Military Reserve. Uncle Bert believed he had no chance to survive. The mortality rate was soaring throughout America, taking far more American lives at home than did the war itself. Dad somehow made it; our family lives could again take off. There was a family tenacity already manifest. This seems to have trickled into the next generation, for I too was tried—by whooping cough (Pertussis) a few years later, in the days before immunization became the rule. By then, we had moved to Highland Avenue in Piedmont. I suppose this was a step up on the social ladder.

Dad did not mind the added distance to work. On the cushy seat of his Pierce Arrow, he was never happier than when behind its wheel. This also turned out to be a family characteristic, as I inherited this joy, pushing it to extremes when I passed the Bondurant High Performance Driving test 60 years later. That story can wait.

Dad's work–call it joy

Lyon Storage and Moving Company was the first of its kind west of the Rockies. Most of Dad's vans were horse drawn. He would be on his way at five o'clock each morning in order to supervise the harnessing and make sure that hooves were healthy. Petro Pine  Ointment, a balsamic salve, was his wonder drug. It went on every sore or abrasion. Its quality of clinging made it work. Where did this come from? Some entrepreneur had stored crates of it and then disappeared, not to return. Dad, always the opportunist, on this occasion got his full money's worth.

Dad thought he was a good judge of horses, until he purchased one that turned out to be blind. A Lyon characteristic again appeared as he made the best of a bad bargain. The blind one became the center horse and the leader in the brace of three. His power surpassed his fellows as he pulled the others with him.

Then, in our first Piedmont year, Dad acquired a motored van. It was a flatbed with a top speed of 12 miles an hour. It could deliver loads on Piedmont's streets, so steep that horses feared to tread. Next came the enclosed van, a bit faster. It rang the death knell for horsepower not enclosed in steel, and finally, Dad acquired the tractor-trailer to end up as an 18-wheeler.

Though Dad loved his horses, it was the horsepower driving the pistons in his Pierce Arrows that thrilled him. He told me that he had owned 17 Pierce Arrows in a row. When the models came out in the twenties, still with cloth tops and celluloid side curtains, he started to acquire these seven-passenger behemoths from Piedmonter Eamon of Eamon Olives. He paid $5,000 for each car with its lifetime warranty. After only one year, the Pierce was barely broken in. Soon Dad hired a local company, Gillig, now a nationally known bus company, to put on the first closed top. It was of patent leather and with sliding windows. These cars, with the life-sized lion from the office window on the hood, led many a downtown parade, Dad at the wheel. What a dandy he must been! And when another year went by, the Pierce

would end up in Yosemite Valley as a tour bus with many years yet to go. Sadly, the lifetime warranty did the company in. Studebaker bought it and allowed a slow demise, hastened by WW II, when its unique aluminum engine blocks were melted for arms. Finding Dad's car in a show today is unlikely. My love of cars can't be hereditary. It was acquired, like so many wondrous things we are given by our parents.

I become my brother's keeper

There was a strict rule in our house directed at me, age five, and Ted, age four. Our scooter must never leave the upper driveway, for its course of some 60 feet to the street below was steep. Ted broke the rule. I called out, "Bruder gone down the driveway." Who was punished? Not Ted, but Dick. I had been informed that I was "my brother's keeper." This rule is embedded deep within me. I would repeatedly find that it would extend well beyond such a narrow family designation in life ahead.

So, what was my trial at age five? The whooping cough, Pertussis, hit with a vengeance. I remember long days in the dark in my upstairs room on Highland with shades pulled as I hacked away and scared even my doctor. The decision? We must move to a warmer, drier climate. The change in our lifestyle made no difference as another Lyon characteristic surfaced. The decision was prompt and action just as prompt. Mom and Dad sold the house, and we moved, lock, stock and barrel, to Sunol, some 50 miles away. A family characteristic was becoming firmly embedded in this son. Just assemble the facts, decide, and "Do It Now." I had been given the blessing of being able to almost unconsciously daily assemble facts, shunting aside emotions, and thus being prepared to make the required decision without a moment's hesitation. Was preparing as an engineer, then a doctor, an early subconscious decision?

We move to the country to help me live

Sunol was a child's heaven. We slept in a massive, screened outside

4

porch. Each day we had miles of free walking space through fruit trees and berry bushes bursting with goodies asking to be picked. I can't say it was that easy for Mom, because the cooking was entirely in her hands. I guess I should have felt sorry for Dad and his long commute each day on narrow winding roads through hamlets that now are extended cities, but by then, even in my tender years, I knew Dad was in seventh heaven behind the wheel of his Pierce Arrow. He always had a towline available to give a helping hand to someone out of gas or in a ditch. I am sure those driving hours were his time to think and plan, his eyes never leaving the road, alert to every nuance.

Apparently I recovered my strength after six months in Sunol. Dad found a cottage in an abandoned nursery just one mile from the tiny hamlet of Danville. It was closer to Oakland, and the highways were easier to navigate. We promptly moved in. Of course, moving was duck soup: Lyon was the mover. Mom was now cooking in a cramped kitchen as she made the most of natural food sources all around. Dad would usually drive the Pierce to Saranap—yes, that was its name—a station on the fringes of what would soon be Lafayette. Then he would take the comfortable Sacramento Short Line electric train through the long tunnel in the Berkeley Hills, landing him close to his office in the just completed Lyon warehouse, its clock tower a landmark. It now seems like a toy as the Warren Freeway brushes it to the north. I remember Dad, still in his thirties, telling the powerful three in Oakland—Capwell and Taft of department store wealth, and Tribune newspaper mogul Joseph Knowland—that the city should dig another tunnel through the hills for automobiles. Their reaction? "If we do that, people will move to the country." Dad's rejoinder was, "They are going there anyway. If you don't build the tunnel, they won't come into the city and buy in your stores." Prophetic? You bet. Another Lyon characteristic was showing up: an ability to recognize and assemble emotion-free facts that kept Dad seeming to be well ahead of his time, most of the time. This is not always a blessing, I have since learned.

My dad

Dad's story really began when he graduated from Oakland High School. He was the rare one who chose to go to college. The University of California was close by. There he was known as the calculator guru, and was pictured that way in the yearbook of 1906. One day I asked Dad why he chose to go to college in a time when the trades were flourishing. He said, "I wanted to get an equal start with the best." Thus it was that, in the moving and storage industry, he and the Bekins brothers all were college educated and led the field throughout the country, especially when they became founders of such long distance moving companies as Allied and Bekins. Dad often mentioned that small, local competitors, almost always restricted to a van or two, did not have the advantage that education provided, but Dad would always be there with a helping hand. Thank goodness they had the altruistic guidance of men like Dad, who cherished competition but demanded it be the best it could be.

It was in Danville that I first tasted school, a walk one mile to the east. I would saunter back and forth each day with schoolmates recently immigrated from Mexico. They had already picked up American English and conversation was rich. We all carried lunch boxes and Mom would load mine with goodies. My first grade teacher was Ruth Sorrick. I learned later that I was the only blue-eyed blonde in her room of twenty or so, and I was in hog heaven, for we all were encouraged to think and learn. My classmates were alert and friendly. I think that had a tremendous influence in making me so unconscious of ethnic backgrounds. Their dark complexions and jet black hair were truly beautiful, and how we laughed and played together.

One day Mom was in the center of Danville, moving toward the bank to make a withdrawal. She was driving the Pierce that day. She saw a man run out of the bank with a bag in his hand, presumably full of stolen cash. The alarm was sounded and the sheriff commandeered the powerful Pierce to make chase. Did the robber get away? I think so. He might not have, had Dad been at the wheel.

That was an idyllic world I know now, but I don't have to look back and wish I had understood that at the time. Why? Well, my parents constantly demanded we appreciate the joys and blessings of each day as just that—taking nothing for granted. It is the same for me today. If these are God's gifts, I say, "Thank you." If these are Man's gifts, I say, "Thank you for Man."

We return to the city

After two years in the country it was time to return to the big city and its challenges. Just before picking up stakes, my teacher, Miss Sorrick, became Mrs. Lamborn. This blond, blue-eyed "teacher's pet" was the ring bearer and, for the first time, I found myself playing hide and seek—should I say flirting?—with Jeanie, Ruth Lamborn's niece and my companion

going down the aisle. I didn't give in to her entreaties for a kiss. Guess I blew it, and that would not be the last time.

By this time Dad's business was booming. We moved blocks up the social ladder to Piedmont and 306 Sheridan, an English two-story house on a narrow lot, surrounded by more imposing residences. It was just a mile from Havens Grammar School and Piedmont High School, all on level ground, easy to negotiate on bicycle, roller skates or scooter. It's hard to believe now that a small bike was then a curiosity. Dad, always resourceful, managed to find a much-used one. Ted and I, as well as the rest of the neighborhood, became cyclists by sitting on the bike and pushing off from the curb. It was self-instruction at its best.

How did we live? Mom was able to have wonderful, supportive help with cooking and cleaning, as well as demand a little discipline for three obstreperous boys. Twelve quarts of milk were delivered each day, and the despised cod liver oil was replaced with a delicious, expensive mix called Kepler's Malt Extract. Mom was presented with her new revolutionary electric mixer, the KitchenAid. It was supposed to do everything. Applesauce was its number one product, and I developed the trick of always mixing it in my milk, something I still do today. And then there were the dishes to be washed and dried. I have had a lifetime familiarity with this because it was our chore after each meal and continued to be my chore, among others, when I hashed in the dining hall of Encina in my first Stanford year. There I set the tables for 24, served, and then after setting up for the next meal, went through the dishwashing routine. We hashers, for the most part athletes, would sweep through the swinging doors, our trays with 24 glasses of milk balanced above with one hand, while the other hand opened the swinging door. It must have been like a ballet, I think, looking back at the wonders of being just a youth.

Why bring up this mundane dishwashing activity? It was because I learned something else from my Dad on how to get out of an odious job at home. Mom would say, "Harvey, get in here and help the boys." Dad would roll up his sleeves, grab a plate, somehow then let it slip and crash to the floor. He had made sure it was not one of Mom's cherished Dresden cups or saucers. Mom, then suckered, would exclaim, "Harvey, you're always so clumsy. Get out of here." A couple of winks by Dad at us boys, and he was back to his newspaper. I haven't had the opportunity to try that stunt. Could it be that my coordination won't allow it? I doubt that, particularly after dropping and smashing a priceless Sevres cup, when I broke the packing rules as a "packer" on a moving job. I had been told more than once by an experienced packer to always open a package over the barrel so if something slipped it would have a soft landing. The owner of the cup was a doll, thankfully, but the price of the cup made the lesson stick. I was beginning to realize that mentors were always around if one just listened.

How did Mom cope with the energies of three boys, keeping them out of the trouble that seems the outlet for so many without homes and caring parents? Well, one of the prices paid was our furniture. We would wrestle in the front room, older, stronger Dick usually putting Ted on his back with a hammerlock, until Bruce, five years younger than me, insisted on getting his share of the action. It wasn't long before he would then hammerlock me from behind with Ted down, thereby freeing Ted and winning the day. Then we would take the long footrest from the front of the fireplace and place it in the middle of the floor. Because there were three steps into the room, the top of the steps was ideal for a running flying leap onto it. Needless to say, its springs rapidly flattened, and rather than get a new replacement, Mom faced reality and kept the target in place until two of us were off to college.

Bruce, with his living-room strength, had the serenity we would all like to have. It came to the point that the Havens School bully—an older sixth grader—challenged Bruce. He immediately found himself vanquished as he was pinned to the macadam by Bruce's hammerlock. From that day on, Reg Kittrelle was a pussycat and one of Bruce's best friends. I believe that was the only physical confrontation any of us three boys ever encountered. So, unlike Bill O'Reilly, was our compliance with reality a bad thing? Not at all. Early on we three decided that even if our assailant got two black eyes and lost the match, the price of being the winner with one black eye was a price too high to pay.

Grammar school

What took place in grammar school that might have been a glimpse of what was to follow? Third grade teacher Mrs. Haas, in her Mexican costumes, planted the seeds leading to a lifetime desire to know the outside world. My sixth grade teacher, Mrs. White, believed music should play a major part in our lives ahead. She played and replayed such classics as *Meditation from Thais* and *Night on Bald Mountain*, planting more seeds that have blossomed and enriched my life. Perhaps most revealing of the lifetime ahead was two years in Mrs. Lohse's Latin class. Was this searcher for ways to remember even then fascinated by the stems from which our western languages have sprung?

Our first and last larceny

One of my most vivid memories of those years took place when I was 13 and Ted 11: the Charleston candy bar incident. Dad always gave us a 25-cent allowance each week to be used for whatever we wished, such as a Saturday trip to the Piedmont Theater, which required a streetcar ride to and from. Candy that would rot our teeth was not on the accepted list.

Dad had a second method to dispense the nickels and dimes we required to take the streetcar all the way to Oakland for the essentials, such as a visit to the dentist—a brown, leather purse tied up with string. Ted and I knew very well that we were cheating, even stealing, when we found ourselves taking more than was needed; we were breaking Dad's trust. How could this occur when both of us clearly knew the difference between right and wrong? Mr. Springman, the pharmacist and proprietor of our one pharmacy, also wondered about this. He phoned my Dad in his office early one morning saying, "Mr. Lyon, have you been allowing the boys to buy chocolate bars on their way to school?" Thirty minutes later Dad appeared in Principal Harry Jones's office. He had a chore to perform and would like to take his two boys home.

Into each classroom he marched and, with finger beckoning, led us to the car and home and upstairs where the looted bank was checked and the guilt assured. We happily admitted culpability: Let's pay up and get off the conscience hook.

Dad did his needed part. Nothing was said. Down came two pairs of pants, and Dad's hand reddened, hurting as he administered our first real spankings. Our reactions, not spoken, but nevertheless transmitted, were in essence, "Thanks Dad, we cheated. We have paid the price." Thank you for what? No amount of discussion or reasoning was necessary. We were stuck in our transgressions. Convicted, sentenced, punished, and guilt removed, we could get back on stride. If that is corporal punishment, so be it. It works, leaving no doubt as to right and wrong. The debt is paid. Sure beats talking!

Looking back, I have wondered why we didn't just on our own 'fess up. I'm guessing that we were also putting Dad to the test. Did he really mean what he said about honesty and personal responsibility? Having already committed our crime, were we wondering how long it would take for Dad, with his adding-machine mind, to discover the robbery of his "till"? Dad trusted his sons and would never have counted the nickels and dimes each week, anticipating a robbery. It took Mr. Springman, outsider and real friend, to accept the responsibility. How wonderful to have been allowed this mistake, to then pay the bill, once and for all, and clean the slate, no discussion required. Once was enough!

We adjust to high school

Junior high school's two years opened new vistas as Mrs. Grover had us study the world, its peoples and geography. My report on Uruguay lit an interest in the outer world that is just as ardent today. These 7th and 8th grade years were the first steps into high school. Our classes changed radically. Most dramatic was the mingling of students from Beach School in lower Piedmont from working blue-collar families and our top-of-the-world bunch, almost without exception from the moderately well-to-do to the very rich families, consisting of executives on both sides of the Bay. Could one be aware of any difference? I for one could not, and our friendships knew no limitations.

The girls all wore uniforms, as in most private schools. I will always believe that the well-pressed pleated black skirts, and loose white middies made an immense difference, stimulating the boys to dress with the same neatness and without pretense. This is a practice that today should be a starting point for inner-city schools, the government paying for these uniforms that level the playing field and stimulate classroom performance through personal pride.

Yes, we had clubs, but these were for the most part unpretentious. I was a Kimmer, mostly drawn from upper Piedmont. Many of my best friends were Rigmas, from the other side of the tracks, so to speak. I don't remember much competition, save as to the type of soft drink each would serve at parties. As athletes, there was no club loyalty, and if initiations were the same, Ted and I would have hated both. The inane use of the paddle to soften up us new members was primitive. By the time we two had finished our high school years, we had made sure the use of paddles was on the skids. I remember so well that I received some fifty blows—yes, I counted them—and finally turned to my tormentors saying, "You guys might as well quit. My butt is numb and you're wasting both of our times." On the other hand, Ted's fanny was swollen and red. No wonder we condemned the whole thing.

It was clear from the very start that Mom and Dad approved of our determination to treat our companions as we would like to be treated, and that is still the rule. I now think that "empathy" was heavily in our genes right from the start, aided and abetted by my parents, who made sure their sons understood that the most offhand remark must be recognized for the meaning it carried to others.

Forming our views of the world

Looking back, I realize that skin color was never an issue. Takeo Hamamoto was our number one tennis player and greatly loved. He had come to America, surely from a leading family in Japan, and was making his way as a houseboy. To us this was admirable. How I wish I had followed him to the internment camp as the war with Japan began. I never understood why President Roosevelt was not better advised. He should have allowed these wonderful people to return to their homes and, as Americans, to aid the war effort. I understood the need to initially get them off the streets and protect them from militant kooks, but we missed the boat. As the years went by and I worked with Japanese-American nurses, I became convinced that no ethnic group more quickly adapts to our ways. This was buttressed by our later prewar experiences as we traveled the world, Japan our starting point. My point is that our home training left no doubt that our judgments of others, and ourselves, would have only one dimension. This was quite simply *character*. And it is the same for me today.

Piedmont High School daily took me closer to the time I would have to leave the protection of home and community as the step to college must be made. Somehow, I was acutely conscious of the blessings I was enjoying, not really looking forward to college, where the big decisions would be made. Some of my friends were anxious to get away and get started toward clearly-defined careers. Easily, the embryo doctors led the list. Engineers, writers, and artists seemed to follow. I, on the other hand, chose to wait and let the chips of direction fall. I was in no hurry to confront responsibility. I milked each day for all of its worth.

A non-combative world for me as mentors appear

In personal histories, often a great deal of time is given to demonstrating one's ability to court confrontation while not compromising principles. This was not an option for me. I don't remember a single instance of such combat, nor do I remember compromising on principles. We brothers seemed to have sensed from the start that we did not require the approbation of others to follow our inclinations. Combat? Yes, on the basketball court or rugby field, as part of the team. Yet, I saw this as just fun and admired so often the ability of the athlete who was my opponent. I remember being benched in a basketball game with USC when the "almost All-American" center outmaneuvered me for a lay-up basket. I hit him on the fanny with my hand saying, "Nice going, Gale." Coach Dean's advice was, "Get mad!" I didn't know how and stayed benched for the rest of the game.

We Lyon brothers had parents who always took part, to the degree that Dad and Mom were each president of the respective Fathers' and Mothers' Clubs for as long as five years. Didn't anyone else want these jobs? Perhaps, but I never heard a criticism. This pattern of accomplishment extended to Oakland's Children's Hospital, as well as to the local business and charitable organizations, Mom's almost-presidency of the National DAR, and Dad's presidency of the National Warehousemen's Association. Were  we boys impressed? I don't believe so, for we saw our parents just as feeling obligated to be effective in anything thrust upon them. Sounds too good to be true, I guess, but this was an ingredient manifest in most communities in the America of that day, and when our parents funded and thus created the Bruce Lyon Children's Hospital Research Laboratory as a memorial, it was just the natural thing to do, no matter the family largess that was required. The Bruce Lyon Grove of redwoods at the Oregon-California line carries the same message.

Humor was part of our daily fare. At the dinner table Dad would tell us his latest joke, the punch line of which he had already posted in his little black book. He accumulated one book for each year, kept them in his dresser, and then at the end of a long lifetime must have discarded them. They were lost to his boys. No matter; his sons knew almost all by heart, so often did he tell them to illustrate a point. I have that habit today and call them shaggy dog stories, not sure that today's listeners think them at all funny, but Dad was famous in the Bay Area for his fund of jokes. Prominent men such as UC Berkeley President Robert Sproul and Oakland District Attorney Earl Warren would drop in for a story befitting a specific occasion, the latter even as Chief Justice of the United States Supreme Court. His best jokes seemed to be pointed at oneself, demonstrating a kind of humility, I think. I like to believe that this is really the case, because it seems to be familial. Taking oneself too seriously is a tough load to bear.

Dad's booby prize

Sometime in the 1920s, when Dad was president of the California Warehousemen's Association, he went to Florida for a convention, played golf, and came back with the booby prize, a tiny alligator. That little organism somehow made the five-day train trip home. He was kept in the fenced back yard and soon grew large enough to threaten our chow dog, Ching, so Dad made a deal with the owner of the plush Broadway Restaurant in Oakland with its multiple fountains. For several weeks or months he was an attraction there until he started chasing the waitresses. He ended up as the first reptile in the new Oakland Zoo in Montclair, a happy beginning for hopefully a long life from prize to perpetuity, since alligators have long lifespans.

My first mentors, after Mom and Dad

How many of my teachers became mentors for me? What is a mentor? There are teachers from whom we learn, but teachers become mentors when they discern something in one that perhaps lies undiscovered and that must be encouraged to blossom.

First, there was Brick Johnson, a Scot if there ever was one, so strong, demanding, and principled. His bagpipe band was the real thing. I practiced on my chanter by the hour, but was never available to play the pipes because I was on the playing field, being encouraged on by them. Brick was also my Sunday School teacher. He characterized Christ in a way that has impacted me to this day. He said, "Christ was a powerful man, not as he appears so often in art. Could any of you in the best of condition carry that cross to the top of the hill?"

Brick was co-coach with Sam Moyer, and he believed that men are made on the field of competition—football in this case. There was another believer, Harry Jones, our principal. Each year he would tell the 1,200 of us the story of his exploits as a teacher in a tiny Midwestern school, where student ages ranged from 12 to 22, all in one room. He had a physical confrontation or two and quickly decided there must be a better way. Pop Warner, now legendary, had written a small book entitled *The Forward Pass*. Book in hand, Mr. Jones found two receivers, and a boy-man who could throw the ball. For three years this tiny school won the state championship, finally taking on the collegiate normal schools and defeating them by scores into the nineties.

What was the secret of such success? It was a combination of surprise and habit. It took years for the surprise to end, as habit gave way to a better way to play. What was the lesson for me? Although we pride ourselves in adapting to something new each day, in fact change is more likely to be slow. It would be years before I would test this principle.

It was Principal Jones' contention that it was on the football field where one becomes a man. I was in the 10th grade, beginning to sprout to an eventual 6'2" with the 126-pound weight of a beanpole, really little different from a newborn colt. The appeal to manhood was so effective that ninety boys showed up, and ninety uniforms were filled. I succumbed and was given the ninetieth uniform, a ratty affair, putting me on the ninth and last string. I was bottom of the line, but that seemed to be not a factor, for we all had to learn how to tackle and block. It would have been wiser to send me on the run with the order to catch, but, no, first I had to learn to tackle. Guess who was my first runner? It was the Coach's son, first-string fullback Dick Moyer, 5'6" and a rolling ball of sheer, hard muscle.

I promptly decided I really wasn't ready yet to be a man. My young, growing, loosely-protected bones would shatter just to have Dick Moyer look at me. I ran to the sports house and into Coach Brick's office, shedding my suit, claiming cowardice. To my amazement, he laughed and said, "Take off that suit and go up to the gym and grab a basketball." That did it. I wasn't a coward after all, and he had better plans for me as he directed me to the sport that would make me All-Conference center and then a teammate of the man who would forever change the game, Angelo "Hank" Luisetti.

Beyond Mom and Dad, mentors like Brick were just beginning to appear. I also had quite wonderful teachers, not in the roles of serious mentors. There was Mrs. Beebe, who tried without success to make me write using the Palmer full-arm method. I would get a B at best. I could not satisfy Mom's desire to see me with all A's to make her sure I was as smart as my buddy, Albert Rowe. He, like his famous dad, a pioneer in Allergy, was on his way to being a doctor. I made a deal with Mrs. Beebe: If she would promise not to watch me as I wrote with hand motion alone and grade me instead on written results that deserved an A, I could please Mom. Once straight A's reached home, Mom was satisfied. I said, "Mom, that's it." I could return to imperfection, and did.

Dr. Niemann, my chemistry teacher, although full of imaginative presentations, could not pierce my inability to memorize easily. The need to use trial and error in constructing an equation left me cold. Even then trial and error was the last thing I wished to use in speeding my understanding of truths that would guide my life. Mr. Banker, historian, was also a fine source of historical facts, but didn't quite have the enthusiasm to give facts life.

Mr. Weingarten was the winner, as far as I was concerned. Algebra was my joy. It didn't have to be memorized. Understanding it just required common sense, my long suit, conditioned by a dad who exuded it. Geometry was a close second as it stimulated the small bit of the artist in me, suspending Algebra in the third dimension of space, but then came Trigonometry. I didn't know then why it was so difficult. Years of experience later revealed that I had a serious deficiency, by teaching standards. I couldn't memorize what I couldn't quickly understand. A formula demanding a complex of plusses and minuses all square-rooted had to be taken at face value. I simply couldn't do it, and this deficiency would later play a major role in directing me to my life's work. The Process Mind was beginning to manifest itself.

And then there was Assistant Principal Bolenbaugh, who installed me as head of the Student Council, charged with discipline and moral issues. He knew even then that I would be unlikely to win the popular vote and hold an elective office. That had already transpired when Chaffee Hall, un-athlete of the year, dearest friend, and the *Daily* editor, whipped me in the election for the most coveted job, Commissioner of Entertainment. The irony and final nail in my political coffin was the fact that Dad was providing most of the entertainers. I would seem to be the logical choice, but Dad performed the same service for Chaffee.

Mr. Seagrist, our Biology teacher, made the course fun for me as it was a challenge to understand physiological laws that guided so much of our lives. The quick memorizers did their thing and scored well. I, on the other hand, had the privilege of working to understand. I guess my A was well deserved. I was beginning to accept that I had to understand principles and theorems before I could commit them to a memory that wasn't overnight but would likely last a lifetime. In retrospect, this has turned out to be the case.

Mr. Hampton, who taught Physics and was always a little absentminded, never learned of the risks I blithely took when I chose as my term project, *chromium plating*. This required a combination of chemicals that produced toxic cyanide gas as an end-product. How to get rid of this? In our basement, I boiled my mixture under a large funnel and hose, directed outside to exhaust the gasses. I survived the process and received an A. You can be sure I kept the matter to myself, and accepted that at times a little bit of luck is a very good thing. I shudder now as I look back at my innocence.

Before and after "The Crash"

I well remember one day in 1928 in our house on Sheridan that Dad had stopped me as I was leaving the front bathroom. He stepped in, closed the door, and said, "Dick, I have to tell someone. Your Dad is a millionaire." Guess I must have said, "Nice going." I recall that I was not impressed, for our living habits were wholesome and not changing. Soon after, however, we moved into what I called "The Big House" at 25 Crocker, with a portecochere and all the fixings, on the most prominent corner in Piedmont: Crocker and Wildwood.

As I started Junior High School, the Crash of '29 began to take its toll, but three years earlier, as Dad prospered, he had bought the Abbott house and spent $25,000 renovating it. It was a spacious colonial mansion, its interior almost entirely paneled with dark mahogany brought from the Far East. It was impressive—but oppressive. Off-white paint covering this magnificent wood made it light and airy. Each of us three boys had our own bedroom and bath for which we chose the colors. Mine was an impressive green with black trim. In a way, we reveled in our new luxury, but the price included much garden work for us and Mom. The garden work paid 25 cents an hour, pure wealth. Dad, with his usual foresight to cover the improbables of the future, rented the 306 Sheridan house as a backup. It was just two blocks away.

Life in our mansion on Crocker called for more help. In Piedmont grandee style, my parents hired our first Chinese cook, Lee Wong. Loyal, pigtailed servants were fixtures in the homes of most of the truly wealthy families. He never took a day off, living in his small kitchen side room. Can one imagine this change in lifestyle for three boys brought up in a single desk-filled room with one closet, three beds on a porch, and within 200 feet of trolleys that constantly banged as they switched night and day? In truth, if there was a quiet holiday, the silence would awaken us with a "What's that?" from one of us. Our second new household member was a "house boy" from the Philippines. It was serene for a few weeks, but when Lee went after the house boy with a kitchen knife, we realized that Lee was quite enough, and the chores of making beds and Saturday cleaning were back in place for the three of us.

I don't think anyone around us took much notice of the new inhabitants until Dad saw beautiful white cutout deer lighting up a Christmas display on Piedmont's most imposing lawn just a few blocks away, that of Wallace Alexander. Dad got an idea immediately: He brought the two life-sized paper maché lions from his warehouse, and we placed them appropriately on the lawn beside a fir tree. A scattering of make-believe snow completed the tableau. Cars going by almost crashed with drivers astonished at Africa in the cold. That did it! Mom ordered Dad to cease and desist, especially when someone accused her of advertising *Let Lyon Guard Your Goods*.

Almost overnight, Dad descended from millionaire status to a debtor of a million dollars. Dad had invested heavily in Oakland prime property. The banks had been too lenient in allowing loans that within a matter of weeks were more than the properties were worth as their values plummeted. How did Dad survive such times? He went to each bank and, in so many words, said, "If I am forced into bankruptcy, you will get nothing. If I agree to pay you 50 cents on the dollar in installments, you will gain the most, and perhaps I will survive." They were convinced. Over the next nine years Dad, bag in hand, collected moneys from such as the parking lot he had owned next to the Paramount Theater, in order to whittle away at his debts.

"Home" returns to 306

As the world came tumbling down, we moved again, back to 306 Sheridan, lock, stock and barrel. It seems odd, but I don't remember much about the move. It just seemed that we were really home again. The small family room again was graced by the Philco radio, but the furniture breathed a sigh of relief as our energies, now more channeled, did not include wrestling. It was back to the single three-boy bedroom, now a little smaller as we had all become bigger, but the fit was easy, and life for us just took up where it had left off. Mom no longer would be weary from the incessant demands of a large garden. We boys had a smaller lawn to weed and mow. Our weekly stipends of 25 cents were not cut, but the chances for added earnings became limited.

At the same time, Dad was each day making his deposit in the bank to pick away at each loan. That took nine years of daily humbling. The memory is fresh today of Dad stopping me in the rough at the brow of Orinda Country Club's fourth hole. As it had been that day in the bathroom, Dad said, "Dick I must tell you something. Your Dad doesn't owe a single cent to anyone." If his eyes didn't tear at that moment, I would be surprised, for my eyes tear today just with the thought.

Dad saved Lyon Storage and Moving Co. with the help of $17,000 from grandmother Richards, then occupying our guest room. It was a mighty tight squeeze. Still nursing his pride, Dad could now afford only an Oldsmobile. For a year he parked around the block in hiding. He believed he must maintain the mantle of success. I suspect it was a help. Several Piedmont friends took their lives for insurance support for families. Mr. Hamby lost his magnificent grocery store as the wealthy ran up immense bills, never repaid until too late.

True Grit, as we look back

Dad demonstrated the truth of his lessons to his sons as he took his beatings without a moment of self-pity. I never heard a complaint as he recognized his poor judgment, although events that took place had been correctly anticipated by only a few. However, an event just before The Crash throws light on the values he passed on to his sons, these values having a price.

In 1927, two years before The Crash, Dad decided to expand Lyon Storage and Moving Co. by adding a second unit in San Francisco. Things must have been going well, for this was the prosperous run-up to 1929. He acquired perhaps the choicest property in San Francisco. It was directly across from the City Hall in the Civic Center. Today it is hard to believe that finding and acquiring such a nugget was possible. The warehouse was to be the finest in America and a standard for fire proofing advances that assured storage safety. The foundation was complete and the first floor underway, with $10,000 worth of steel already delivered. Then the axe fell. Horace Clifton, chairman of the San Francisco Opera Board knew that a fine orchestra would remain a dream without a true Opera House. It was now "put up or shut up," all set in motion by Dad's foresight. The city fathers gave in. The property was condemned for public use, but Dad was offered any other available property he would choose.

In the meantime, Dad had second thoughts about this new venture. Crossing the Bay meant lost time on the ferry twice daily—no bridge then—and this commute time had become precious, for it invaded time at home with his family. I believe he quietly sighed with relief, reclaiming the funds, happy to be a big guy in (then) a little pond.

The story now takes an unexpected twist, for this was the heyday of property and stock market values. He took the funds and bought TransAmerica stock, believing it golden at a value of over $200 a share. Over the next two years, it steadily worked its way down. Only when it reached $100 did he ask his sons' opinions, our ages to 7 to 12. Our decision was unanimous: "Sell." Dad didn't take our advice, and then watched TransAmerica plunge to zero. That was when the full impact of The Crash hit home. No tears from Dad. He would just "gut it out." Lessons for his boys? You have only yourself to blame when things go badly. Quietly, bite your lip and get on with making the very best of it.

Life-preserver golf

It would seem that a sport would just provide delightful memories throughout our growing years, but in our case, golf was something quite different. It came close to being a way of life, teaching us lessons that would help us through difficult times yet ahead.

In his prime, Dad had been a founder of Orinda Country Club, a gem in the hills just one half hour away from home. We three boys and Dad started playing golf as we reached age ten. This was a family affair from the start. The Sunday picnic on our lot, intended for a home someday, was followed by the Lyon eighteen-hole foursome, Mom biding her time reading and knitting. Dad, even with all of his worries, kept our game a ritual.

Ted and I became proficient golfers, making up the second pair on the high school team. We never lost a match. It was years later that I recognized why. Younger brother Ted, with his consistent, upright, finely-honed swing went right down the middle. I rarely was able to best him. I, on the other hand, was a bit wild, but long. In our matches, at about the fifteenth hole, we would begin to pull away. Why? Because our opponents would start to spray their shots as they tried to get the longest drives. I would often do the same, while Ted went down the middle and we won the closing holes. Our golfing buddies couldn't understand why we wouldn't be intent on competing with them more often and thereby improve our games. We never offered an explanation. We just played as a family together.

The finale to all this is that when Dad's world came crashing down, his sons were his shock-absorbers—always there and ready to go. The country club should have been one of the casualties, but our golf therapy for Dad would have been denied. Was someone looking after us, we wondered, for Dad's founder's lifetime membership demanded no dues, and our locker was $1 a month. Golf balls? No problem. After the Sunday game, we trekked back to the thickets lining the course. Ted somehow found just new balls. I found mostly "rocks," but we shared everything, of course.

To this day, golfing buddies can't understand my attitude towards the game. It is the same in other one-on-one sports, such as tennis and swimming. There must be something wrong with me, if I am to judge from the many books on individuals where winning is the name of the game. It is true that I didn't like to lose so often to brother Ted, but at the same time I gained no joy out of being the winner. To this day, this intent is the same. I prefer to come out even, both of us having played a fine game. Many times, as I faced a one-foot putt to win, something inside would trip my hand to make me miss. Had the putt been necessary for me to secure a tie, I would calm myself and sink it, usually. We would be even. My joy has always been in the game that I played within myself.

My future: doors kept open ahead

At fourteen, I began to think about what I would like to do with my life. Our year studying the outer world in geography class in junior high school rang the bell. The outside world, so far away, seemed almost inaccessible, but it beckoned. I would join the Foreign Service and see that world. What could give me a helping hand? Practical from the start, I imagined diplomats in white tropical suits, long pants and all, cavorting on the tennis courts. Golf then was still in its diplomatic infancy. A first step then would be to become competent in tennis, and then I could be a desired partner on the courts when ambassadors needed talented partners to win their contests.

This was later borne out when Dr. Bill Smart, dear friend and champion golfer, as a mere Lieutenant would, in innocence, walk through the officers mess on his aircraft carrier in golf attire. His golf cleats clanged on the deck before he stepped into the Admiral's gig for a game that day, and we were at war!

Berkeley Tennis Club was a major center of great tennis. Locals Helen Wills and Dorothy Jacobs were world champions. I took the streetcars, changing as necessary, and met with the tennis pro, Mr. George Hudson. He agreed to give me ten lessons at $4 a lesson. I had $40 from weekend gardening jobs. The ten weeks went rapidly by. I was given a firm basis for a classic free-swinging game, although there was no time in between to practice. Nevertheless, my game was good enough to make the third pair of Piedmont's team, while the golf and basketball teams were not neglected.

So, what is my point in telling this story? It is to strive to be taught only by the best, right from the start. If it requires long rides on the trolley cars, so what. Just make it work. Do It Now.

Away from home at college and the value of the name Lyon

Graduation meant the first major change in a life pattern so ordered thus far. In 1934, it was time to break the comforting and ever-encouraging bonds of home. What did I wish to be? I hadn't the slightest idea, for my talents seemed so ordinary in the face of my buddies with gifts in music, art, and writing. We were confirmed "Golden Bears," and UC Berkeley was to be the next step in preparing for my life's work. At this time, I was high-point man, the center on a winning basketball team. I had earned All-Conference status, so, along with ten others originating in the western states, I was offered a scholarship at Stanford. Dad's doubts about financing my college education without my living at home were relieved.

Then came the June surprise: Coach John Bunn called to say that the Board of Athletic Control denied my scholarship because the name Lyon of Lyon Storage and Moving with its slogan, *Let Lyon Guard Your Goods*, was too well known. Stanford could not be seen to be subsidizing wealth. This was in the early days of Dad's recovery. Technically, he was still broke. I faced Dad on the back porch that evening.

"Dad," I said, "How much is the name Lyon worth?"

Dad retorted, "What do you mean by our name having worth? Give me a figure?"

"Dad, is it worth $345 a year?"

"What's that?"

"That is the tuition at Stanford for a year. You give me the scholarship, and I'll work my way through."

Dad said, "OK. It's a deal."

Thus, the Lyon Scholarship was created. He paid up and I worked, hashing at Encina Hall as a freshman and then hashing again at sororities. I also worked for a small government grant doing bookwork and as a private contractor washing well-to-do boys' cars. I did odd jobs in the summer, and in my last year all needs were met as house manager of my fraternity.

CHAPTER

2.

I Go to College

Stanford beginning

My first quarter of the academic year was a difficult one. In order to get by financially, I lived for three months in a small room with a bath at the back of Coach Bunn's home. I never had a meal there, let alone saw the dining room. Its distance from the campus meant arising early in order to hash at Encina Hall, followed by a busy day of classes and basketball practices. Not having a room at Encina Hall kept me from getting into the swing beyond making new friends on the court. Weekends at home were a refuge.

Something had to change! Dad agreed to help with costs as I moved into Encina Hall in January and could then take part in campus life, my hashing duties now next door. I would find it a joy in my sophomore year to live in the fraternity house, my home for the next three years, as well as the dining table later during the months on campus in medical school.

I play basketball with the coming star, Angelo "Hank" Luisetti

Hank Luisetti proved to be all that was expected and a joy to be with on the team. From the start, the competition was intense. As the days wore on, our diminutive, feisty, freshman coach tried different

27

combinations. I usually ended up with Hank as the other forward or as center.

We started our season in Auburn, heralded there as the great team we were on our way to becoming, winning all but one of our games. That game I most remember, for it was our opening encounter with the Cal frosh. We gained our first dose of what a "hot" team could do. Cal players, such as Chet Carlisle and Ed Dougery, couldn't miss no matter from where they threw the ball. We tried three kinds of defense yet lost miserably. The irony was that each year for the next three, the same "hot" night occurred at Cal, so that almost our only losses were these

and they were clearly won by Cal, to their absolute joy. I remember so well Dougery just standing there and tossing the ball while laughing in my face. Strangely, in all my Stanford years, I don't remember a hot Stanford team night. If Hank couldn't hit, he would shoot anyway, and then on a first or second follow-up on the shot, ram it in, something no longer possible with the giants under the basket.

Hank was the consummate basketball player, the equal of the modern stars, such as Michael Jordan, who seem so superior. This is largely because of their freedom to take three steps instead of two, to palm the ball in the dribble, and to strike the basket rim as they dunk. I have the clipping telling of the foul I incurred as my wrist touched the net on a lay-up. I guess "white guys could jump." The dunk changed that, not to the advantage of the game. I saw Hank make the first dribble behind his back as he left the All American USC captain, Hal Dornsife, just standing there, then throwing up his hands as though asking the crowd what they would do. Hank's defensive moves were unmatched even today.

Engineering to Hygiene to Engineering

Now the awakening! My first semester was a disaster, for Descriptive

Geometry turned out to be Trigonometry all over again, yet magnified. Professor Butter made me feel just "too dumb to get it," and I had no intention of continuing if I couldn't get it, so I dropped my major and switched to Hygiene, at least to get my breath and regroup.

At that low point, I pinned Mom with the question, "What was my IQ on the Terman Test?" Mom hesitated, but I was not to be denied. She said it was 136. What a relief! I wasn't anywhere near a genius at 140 or above, but was in a range where I hoped sheer determination, persistence, and hard work could make anything possible. I let things go at that until—a miracle? Yes, I think so as I look back.

Dr. Harold Bacon (thank goodness, not Butter again), Professor of Mathematics, was the timer at our freshman games. He had heard that I had dropped out of Engineering. As a freshman, I was playing forward with Hank Luisetti, trying to emulate his one-hand push shot that changed the game. Dr. Bacon asked me to go back into Engineering and repeat the first year of math with him, and somehow we would make it go. He backed up his promise, each week devoting several hours to coaching what I know now was my Process Mind to make sense of Descriptive Geometry, and Differential and Integral Calculus. A key boost to my confidence came when I earned one of the three A's in Integral Calculus. The other two A students were in another realm, I believed. They had done the assignments in an hour and were playing pool when I asked for help.

Yes, HWDP—Hard Work, Determination, and Persistence—could make the difference. I never would doubt that again.

A big step that took years to understand

Now let's jump forward to cement the contention I have just made. My Hydraulics course, considered the most demanding, both in substance and in performance, was taught by Dr. Hedburg, a no-nonsense guy. As I walked into the final exam room, I was blown away by the activity. Students were burning up their slide-rules, making calculations seem easy. I panicked.

I asked Dr. Hedburg, "May I go to the House and do my exam,

please. My head is spinning."

"Of course." We both knew that no book could help.

Four hours later I turned in my Blue Book. I commented, "I think I have flunked the course."

His rejoinder, "We'll see." Two days later the Blue Book arrived with an A on it.

I went to the engineering corner and said to Dr. Hedburg, "I think you should look at this. Your corrector must have made a mistake."

Dr. Hedburg said, "There is no mistake. In fact, you got the highest grade in the course."

"Please, Sir, how could that be when I really didn't know what I was doing?"

"Well, you *derived* every equation."

This statement meant nothing to me at the time. Of course I was thankful for this judgment. There was perhaps something worthwhile yet ahead. It took over sixty years for me to understand the prediction of that day. It was my Process Mind at work. It would pursue its course throughout my professional life and even after. It would only be in the "after" of retirement and time for contemplation that I would strive to understand this Process, in order that others like me with HWDP could early on recognize their possibilities and then realize their full potentials. The "Straight A's" would not be able to keep up.

CHAPTER

3.

1936: Around the World

Grandmother Richards takes over

In the spring of my freshman year, as our Luisetti team took all the honors, my beloved Grandmother Richards quietly passed away as her kidneys failed, the end point of scarlet fever acquired in the waters of Sutro Baths near the Golden Gate. She had been living with us for sometime. I had many talks with her, for I was becoming a history buff. Her tales about the Old South and the Civil War never tired me. Gram knew I had a dream, quite impossible to achieve, of riding a bicycle through Europe, so far away from home and family. Air travel was then restricted to pioneering Pan American flying boats to Hawaii and South America. The telegraph was the only reliable means of direct communication and not available everywhere. So, dream on Dick—no charge—as you still have the Foreign Service in your prospects.

Gram's Will made this dream come true. Ted and I were each to receive $800 that could only be spent riding bicycles in Europe. There was no backing off from this commitment, and there was a time frame dictating "now." The year was 1936, and the Olympics would be in Berlin.

Dad and Mom, faced with an obligation that must be met, and frightened, of course, started to plan. Both of them, always making something odious into something good, decided that the $1,600 could be stretched to take us around the world. Dad would make us into Rotary Ambassadors of Goodwill by enlisting the help of Paul Harris, Founder of

Rotary, that was by then established in 57 countries, many on our route. His letter assured our parents that their sons would have helping hands when in need, and further, that two American young men, whose teeth were cut on a Rotary Wheel, could strengthen the ties that bind this organization. Dad sent the letter to the clubs in each major city on our route.

We leave our home for eight months to see the world

The hours riding in the bus to Seattle were the only ones on the trip that were troubled by any apprehension. The enormity of our undertaking was becoming obvious. By the time we boarded the NYK Hiya Maru, our confidence had reestablished itself and our days would be dedicated to planning ahead.

The trip in winter in the subarctic seas was a rough one, our sturdy ship and equally sturdy captain plunging along. The ten passengers made common sense of using first class comforts, returning to second class for meals, there chasing plates as they careened, some to the deck. No one was seasick. There was really no time to sit in a deck chair with nothing to do except respond to the environment.

Japan

Our Rotary involvement began the day we landed in Yokohama. We were met and were squired for three weeks in Japan from Tokyo to Kobe. We spoke to Tokyo Rotary, had meals and nights in Japanese homes, and accompanied young folk to Nikko in the awesome beauty of winter snow-decked Japanese temples. We were taken to Hakone and Miyanoshita in the shadow of Mount Fujiama, stayed at the fabled Tawaraya Ryokan (native hotel) in Kyoto, spent the night with the monks on Mount Koya, and watched the Takarazuka dancers in Kobe, their performance far surpassing anything we had seen at home. In the hands of Rotarians, we believed we were seeing the Japanese world of the future. They were the highly educated, often even royalty, as were Baron and Baroness Togo, dedicated to catching up with the outside world, first discovered in the 1880s as the Emperor Meiji accepted Admiral Perry's challenge. These days would have a profound effect on my thinking when Japan would become the enemy just a few years later. At Stanford, as we prepared for this great adventure, I had taken a course in Japanese history and absorbed it to a degree that my appreciation of its culture made Japan for me much more than just beautiful mountains and seas. This tendency to always look forward and prepare for what might occur would be a staple for my life.

China

The Suwa Maru picked us up at Osaka and steamed towards Shanghai, where Rotary again took over. Fong Sec, the father of Rotary in China and Dad's friend, treated us to the most sumptuous meal we would ever have. It was course after course of traditional and historic delicacies that I doubt can be obtained today. We saw the real China in the narrow alleys behind the burgeoning western world of the Bund. Rotary there was in its infancy, lagging behind Japan.

Back on the Suwa Maru, steaming to Hong Kong, Charlie Chaplin, his beautiful companion Hedy Lamarr, and her chaperoning mother made for a few hours of talk. Charlie Chaplin

proved to be an incisive thinker, belying his character on the silver screen.

Rotary in Hong Kong was a surprise. It still operated in the colonial tradition. There were no Chinese members. We watched our words carefully. A side trip to Canton, with its Ling Nan University and American friends there, took us into the heart of old China. The individuality of the Cantonese left an indelible impression that Canton was in an almost medieval state, more like America in its earliest entrepreneurial days. China was far from being cast in a single mold.

Philippines

On our side trip to Manila, we were in the hands of family friends, the Judge Lockwoods. They made sure we tasted of the always colorful flavors of brightly-painted taxis and rickshaws provided by a people seemingly content with the primitive joys that were soon to change. Rotary was not our host at this stop, and this again was the old colonial world. There were cool mountain retreats for the rich and privileged. We, the latter, played a round of golf in Baguio before going on board ship again, back to Hong Kong to board our liner back to the West.

Singapore, Ceylon, Aden, and Suez

In Singapore, the Rotary President met us to be sure our few hours ashore were well spent. The harbor was a mass of activity, which included boys diving for coins beside the ship. Our colonial world again took over as we had cold drinks and lunch at the fabled Raffles Hotel. The city seemed as beautiful and disciplined as I understand it is today. What do I remember most vividly? It was the tall handsome Sikhs in magnificent tunics, hand directing traffic with a flick of a finger, perhaps an arm wave at most, always unflappable.

It was a short sail to Ceylon, now Sri Lanka. Rotary President Reverend Dr. Nathanialez, met

the ship and treated us to classic tropical fare as we talked with his seven children, all with college scholarships waiting for them in England. We will never forget the hot curry and the cold fruit drinks that spoiled us forever. Curry today is not even a shadow of what it was then. As we embarked, the Reverend presented to each of us a tiny ebony elephant. It rests in front of me today as I remember and write.

The rest of the sail took us through the Gulf of Aden and the Suez Canal. In Port Said we had the opportunity to make a one-day side trip to Egypt. Ted and I both felt that such a short visit was unconscionable for a site so historic. We would take our chances that some day in the future we would give Egypt the respect due it. And, of course, there was the added matter of cost. Our dollars were too precious not to hoard them for the biking days ahead.

Marseilles

The Mediterranean's blue surrounded us the next days as we passed the smoking Stromboli volcano, then made land on Easter morning, docking sounds muted by the music of church bells heralding the day. It was Sunday, and another holiday would follow. All of our only dollars were in my money belt as a Letter of Credit that could not be invaded until the banks would open. Mr. Shallam, old "China Hand" returning for a well-deserved vacation in England, took his Masonry seriously. On learning that Dad was a 32nd degree Mason, he staked us with enough coins to carry us through the holidays.

Once on shore, we were really alone. It would be only in Rome, at least a month away, that we would tap again into Rotary and collect letters from home. Were we apprehensive? Absolutely not. The combination of Ted and Dick was secure.

Marseilles is a hub of the maritime world, and waterfront activity was intense. It was known to everyone but us as the most dangerous section of the city, not to be entered at night under any circumstances. Police control had been given up long before. On returning to our little pension that evening, after visiting bicycle shops, we were asked where we had been. Yes, we had just come through the maritime quarter. Our hostess paled as we described the streets we had just passed through. We had made it not only with our belongings, but also with our lives. This is what that experience told us. It is not where you walk, but how you walk. We two, tall Americans, out of ignorance, had sauntered confidently through the robbers' nest and remained untouched, but we would be alert and not take that chance again. We had used up our luck.

We ride 3,000 miles through Europe

For $22 each, we purchased French light racers with three-speed gears and hand brakes. At home we had been spoiled by coaster brakes. English touring bikes with internal rear Sturmey-Archer gears were still unknown to us and unlikely to be found in France. We turned up our handlebars so as to be able look about as we rode. The drawback was that the hand brake levers were then on top. When squeezed to quickly stop, our shift of body weight forward only increased the squeeze, the brake balance being such that we would pitch forward head over heels and land on our backs. This was hilarious when, one day in Rome, we were riding down steep Via Nationale to its intersection with Via Veneto when the magnificently turned out Carabinieri with a finger flick stopped our traffic flow. Ted and I complied by hitting our brakes simultaneously, flipping and landing on our backs, one on each side. We joined the laughter from all sides, something at which all Romans are very good.

French Riviera first

Our first days biking over the hills to Toulon started to toughen us up. At Le Lavendou, a tiny medieval hamlet on the Mediterranean, we had our first taste of rain. In our beachside pension, after delicious meals, it was a treat to sit and read while looking out on the turbulent sea. The ride then took us through even older Hyères to Cannes and Nice. Did we stare at the scantily clad beauties on the beaches? I don't think so. We were still too busy being absorbed into our own world of make believe.

We watched the Rolls Royces roll up to the Monte Carlo Casino. Somehow, we talked the concierge into letting us do our ogling at the tables, hands firmly in our pockets, as we planned for the intensive ride the next day. It would be east on the Moyenne (Middle) Corniche, and then back on the high altitude Grande Corniche with its tiny historic castle at Eze. We were beginning to really roll.

The next day was Saturday, and we would cycle into Italy. The border is a thousand feet above the city of Menton. There we had our first experience with a border crossing, not shared by busloads of tourists flashing by. More lire? For a deposit on our bikes? It's Saturday and the banks are closed!

Ted stayed at the station while I rode down into Menton. I somehow located the Black Market, took a beating in the exchange, and pedaled back up. These two now bedraggled American boys in shorts and T-shirts could pedal into Italy, keeping out of the way of the roaring busses.

It's Italy

Our first taste of Italy on this weekend included red and yellow flowers and a small square filled with old and young, loafing and dancing as joy seemed to fill the air. This was a welcome change from the sophisticated coolness of the French Riviera. It predicted wonderful days ahead, especially when we were able for, about $10 apiece, to procure railroad seats taking us anywhere and everywhere in Italy. Mussolini was rightly famed for his railroads, always on time, with baths (doccia) available at every main station. A hot shower, soap, and towels were provided. Could we ask for anything more?

With bikes in the baggage car everywhere we went, taken out and ridden for miles through historic sites and wholesome countryside, we kept our legs in reasonable shape. However, our strength was no match for that of the locals. Once we hit the cobblestones that ringed every city and paved main streets in the hamlets, there would be friendly competition as youths came up from behind, challenged us, went by, and then rode away to their homes, always laughing and waving.

We were in the catacombs outside Rome when the Harrison Flannerys, scions of an old well-to-do family in Pittsburgh, asked

us if we would like to go with them to Naples and Pompeii in their new Ford convertible sedan. You can't beat that, and those were fun days. They stayed at the finest hotels, while we wandered through the byways, searching for a reasonable and comfortable pension. They had their *Baedeker* to guide them, but we had something better. It was called the *Hand Me Down*, made available by Holland America Line. It was a paperback with  recommendations for hotels, restaurants with their prices, and also special things to see, all gathered from travelers over the many years. It was our bible and never let us down. So, our searches were always short and the results superb.

Beyond the routine visits to Herculaneum and Pompeii, our climb to the summit of the smoking and burning Vesuvius was truly "tops." I can still remember the guide beseeching us to not go any further, but we did until the hot soles of our shoes said "'nuff." I am guessing our visit to the active volcano may have been among the last, as Vesuvius sleeps these days.

Il Duce appears and so do we

We returned to Rome to find the excitement intense, for Il Duce was to speak from his palace in Piazza Venezia. The war in Ethiopia had ended with Italy the victor and now, with a major African colony, the Roman Empire was reborn. All of the avenues entering the Piazza were packed; there were a million people in front of the candlelit Vittorio Emanuele II Monument.

Ted and I, head and shoulders above most of the crowd, sort of slithered and slid forward until we were just a few of feet away from Mussolini standing above on the portico. "*Il Duce*" was the chant, even as he spoke, his hand always out in salute, while small papers printed with *Il Duce* were scattered by planes close above.

Once he disappeared behind the drapes, many near us seemed to be going somewhere else. We followed to find ourselves in a jubilant parade, ending up at the Quirinale, the King's Palace, on top of one Rome's seven hills.
There was the king himself, Victor Emanuel, saluting the crowd. We returned to our Pensione Juliana, two very tired boys.

What do I remember most about Rome of 1936? The fountains and plazas lined with colorful sidewalk cafes; the stillness and peace as we picnicked in the grass and wildflowers lining the large cobblestones of the Appian Way; the inner, fearful grandeur of the Coliseum as we conjured up gladiators coming through the tunnels to fight to their deaths. That dream was breached when we overstayed, finding ourselves locked in. Much yelling brought the Carabinieri, who laughed at our confinement and didn't take us to jail for breaking the law. Bikes took us to Hadrian's Villa, its trees filled with the songs of birds, and the Villa d'Este in Tivoli, magnificent in the night, as Mussolini prized its lighted pools and falls. We threw our coins in the fountain of Trevi as we left to go north, first to Assisi, and then to Florence, Venice, and Milan, finally leaving the train well into the Alps at Iselle.

This hamlet was really tiny—just an equally tiny hotel over a rushing stream and a train station. True to what we had been promised as we left our bikes at the station in Florence, there they were, ready to go again. Thanks, Benito.

We ride over the Simplon Pass—the first that year

Purely by chance and good luck, we went through customs as the first to go over the Simplon Pass that year. Again, we were at the mercy of the agent, a swarthy, unshaven character out of a Hollywood western, who played his part well as he smilingly cheated us as we exchanged lire for francs. No matter, we were thrilled to be on our way through snow tunnels, alternately walking and riding towards the 6,500 foot summit. However, we miscalculated the availability of food. Our usual habit of buying some vegetables and bread along the way was impossible, for habitations were far away on the mountain slopes where cattle grazed, their tinkling bells music to our ears.

It was the Benedictine Hospice that will forever be engraved on our memories. The Saint Bernards met us. The priest took us in, fed us, and sent us on our way. This was a fairy tale made real. A few coins at the altar hardly covered the joy of that day.

We were sure we were finally in Switzerland. There would be no more haggling over each purchase, and blue-eyed, fair-haired country folk would be our hosts. The next ride would be downhill all of the way to Brig, four thousand feet below. Riding at times with our feet on the bars despite the gravel surface, our joy was brought to a halt when my rear tire went flat. The pastures around were empty and silent, until, from nowhere, our first Swiss friend appeared. Mountain dialects didn't allow any explanation. None were needed. He took out his kit, removed the tire, patched it, and blew it up again, all in one motion, ending as he took off with a smile and a wave. What a welcome to the land we had dreamed of for so long!

The mighty Matterhorn was just ahead. To see it meant a long walk, pushing our bikes on a narrow well-worn mountain path. Cars were not allowed in Zermatt. We went through tiny St. Nicholas and along the meandering stream, wildflowers abounding. Zermatt was just as we had anticipated, a fairyland. We gave no thought to making a climb to the Matterhorn's summit, for that would take days of getting used to the altitude, so the magnificent mountain was just that, from afar. We had to be on our way again.

Then came the rain

The Rhone River Valley was an easy coast downhill, we thought, until the winds from Lake Geneva, sweeping so powerfully up the valley, made us push in low gear for hours to make any headway. Rotary came to the rescue in Geneva, placing us in our first hostel. There we learned the virtues of *café au lait*, along with beer, to be a constant source of energy for the rest of our journey.

Then the rains began. It was the middle of June, one of the rainiest months in Geneva. It poured and poured and poured! After four days of waiting for respite, we purchased sorry raincoats—no parkas then— —and went on the road. The water went in at the collar and out over the shoes. We had to keep riding to stay warm, not hard to do going uphill, but a downhill run would chill us to the bone. After one such chill, I spent the night in Ted's arms, our blankets not effective. I must have been in good shape to have tolerated this.

We rode on through picturesque old Bern to Interlaken, still in the rain, which denied us the awe-inspiring views we had expected and believed we deserved. In Interlaken, the Rotary president, architect Niggli, put us in comfy, warm beds. One day of sunshine let us climb up the valley and the three thousand feet to Mürren (no money for the lift) to see the Jungfrau in all of its grandeur. It, along with Zermatt's Matterhorn, had to suffice for Switzerland's physical beauty. The beauty of its people did the rest.

Our first real country hostel outside of Lucerne gave us a taste of what was to follow. It was full, as was often the case, for most travelers were on the road for a day or two and would stop early. We would ride full days, up to 100 miles if pavements allowed, so we often would check in late and accommodations were likely to be makeshift. This night Ted and I slept on mats in the attic, but the view through the bottle glass windows was compensation enough.

Swiss roads were a joy, and bicycle paths were appearing. However, often we would leave the highway, and push and ride up a side road to gain the full flavor of the land and its people. It was on to Lucerne, where our principal destination was the main park and its famous Lion of Lucerne. He didn't let us down. Then we were on to Zurich and our next Rotary experience.

Zurich Rotary, followed by Munich Rotary, came the closest to our American concept of a Club. Herr Turler, maker of world-recognized watches and Herr Sprungli, a world chocolate king, made us feel at home at the meeting. Sprungli chocolates filled our packs when we left. At dinner in Zurich's finest restaurant, we can never forget the spit-barbecued lamb, again a Rotary gift.

The road to Konstanz in Germany borders the Rhein. Its tiny town, Stein Am Rhein, was and still is a gem not to be missed. Boy Scouts paraded as we came by.

Our border crossing was easy, for the first time. They welcomed blond, blue-eyed Aryans, for they were expecting America to join them in their misguided racial ventures, something we knew nothing of at the time. Then our roadways changed, as paved bicycle paths became common in the more traveled areas.

On the bicycle paths and roads of Germany

Munich Rotary was down to just 26 members from over 200 and glad to survive. As an international organization, only it and the Red Cross were allowed. Rotary's survival was special in that Herr Oberhummer, proprietor of Munich's largest department store, was one of the original eight members providing Hitler's initial support in Munich. I have wondered if his heart was broken in the years that

followed. In his store, he made sure we purchased the correct apparel for young men—Bavarian plumed hats, *hosentrager* (suspenders) and *lederhosen* (sturdy leather shorts), and only in fashion when well-worn. Muncheners rubbed butter into the leather to make it look well used. We chose otherwise, because Bavarian manners might be unacceptable in the other parts of Europe we would traverse. Germany's Rotary, bleeding, was to die slowly.

Riding from Augsburg to Nuremburg, we stopped at Erlangen at its Siemens plant. Its Rotarian manager, Dr. d'Ernst, showed us *die werkes*. Then on to the historic quaint old towns—Rothenburg,

Dinkelsbuhl, Heidelberg, and at the Rhein, Hitler's showcase hostel, Stahleck Castle. Then it was cobblestones again along the Rhein to Bonn, and a smooth highway to Koln where Hitler's *Jugend*, (German youths, boys and girls) were toughening up for what was to be their fate.

This was a serious affair. In contrast to Mussolini's young *Fascisti*, with their small and inconspicuous knives made of rubber, the *Jugend*, who carried large German knives in holsters, seemed to mean business. We did not warm up to our hostel neighbors. We were just glad to have a bed on which to place our *schlafsacks* (envelope-like sheets), and to be supplied with a blanket and a 10-pfennig breakfast of *brot* and *milch* each day. We did not tap into Rotary again as we remained vigorous and healthy, though tired, and felt the need to try and catch up with our schedule that had been disrupted by the rains.

Holland

Our introduction to Holland was five days in the home of a family whose "company town" spinning mill was something Ted and I had known only in books. They seemed a happy lot. We slept in really soft beds. We'll always remember our meals: breakfast meant eggs, anyway we wished them, with a variety of Dutch breads hard to imagine.

A word about the designation "Dutch." We quickly learned not to say Dutch. It was too close to the German Deutsch. "Hollander" it would be from then on.

Biking in Holland was a breeze. Hostels were all run privately and with the feeling of a home. The highest hill was only three hundred feet. Bicycle paths went everywhere, although we preferred to ride on the dikes. We visited Amsterdam, Rotterdam, and then the southern island of Walcheren, where the ferry deposited us in Belgium. The crossing went almost unnoticed, so relaxed were the officials. The ride down the poplar-lined canal to ancient Brugge was a high point for us, but rain met us again on the road to Brussels. It was time to hurry on toward Paris. We were running out of time as we anticipated the fall semester at Stanford for both of us.

Paris

Paris was a turning point. Monsieur Beranger, head of Standard Oil and a friend of a friend, took us in. He gave us his guest room nine stories above his opulent apartment on historic Rue de Lille. We breakfasted with him each day. We were again, as in Holland, temporarily spoiled. He also made preparations for me to fulfill my desire, at that moment, for a foreign service career by enrolling me in the *École des Sciences Politiques*, supposedly the finest preparatory school in the world. I could enter it later on. Rotary again took us in, so to speak, assigning Monsieur Franck to aid us. He spent a good deal of his time complaining that his Coca Cola franchise was not paying off; the French loved their wine. I hope he survived the war, as GI's and their Cokes invaded.

Dick gets the Black Flu in Paris and we race to England

Our Paris visit ended when I started to run a high fever accompanied by nausea. This was new, and we had no desire to be sick under French care. We quickly sold our bikes for $5 apiece. I now think we should have brought them home. We boarded the train to Calais, and then the ferry to Dover, and finally the train to London, where the London physician Rotarian placed us in the Russell Square Hotel and made daily visits. By that time Ted was feeling "not so good," but fortunately good enough to stay by my bedside as I became delirious. What is a delirium to me? It is when brother Ted was "there," for I could see him, but he wasn't *really* there. I doubt this will pass the test as an understandable symptom of the Black Flu that was then starting a murderous toll on the Continent. I guess we brought it to England.

There was one major compensation. It was Henry Hyams,

certified London Cockney, who by definition had been born and lived within the range of Bow Bells Church. Henry attached himself to us on the Dover ferry and never really left our sides. He brought us food every day, and then introduced us to Petticoat  Lane. He taught us many of the cockney "rhyming" slang expressions such as "A Rasberry Tart," equivalent to our "The Bird."

Forty years later, Henry would come to California, determined to see Indians. The best we could do, despite driving him and his wife, Mona, the length of the state, was to send him back to London as a cowboy, all five foot two of him with hat, chaps and boots, as he said, "Hi, pardner," passing unchallenged through customs.

We ship for home, at last

Our three weeks of illness ended up with us in a luxurious country club with its Rotary members. With returned appetites and wonderful meals and rest for several days, enough time was left to see Windsor Castle and Stratford-Upon-Avon, the wonders of Hyde Park, and the Tower of London, before shipping out on the Cunard steamship Berengaria for home. Our status was just above "steerage," but as was our experience during the whole trip, we were with the folks who really made the world turn.

When New York loomed on the horizon, at the bow Ted and I were in tears. We reminisced and agreed that coming home to America, its people, its freedoms, and its optimism was a gift unknown anywhere else. However, there is a price, for as we spread our largess, we cannot expect to be loved or even liked by those who are the receivers. Therefore, in order to be concerned for others and generous, we must above all be powerful and never feel guilty because of it.

Knowing how our dad operated, we expected him to be on the dock to greet us and take us home. In that day, Dad would have had to make the five-day train trip to New York. We looked at the crowds below, and no Dad. Oh hum, what's new? We'd make do and somehow find our way home with the few dollars left. Bulky suitcases in hand, we went down the gangplank and started for the street. As we passed the welcomers at First Class, there was Dad. He always expected the best for his sons. In a few minutes, we were gorging on milkshakes at Walgreen's Drugs.

Dad purchased a used Buick, one of the most powerful ever built, and we roared home. There we put pounds on fast, and recovered the strength that would enable Ted to be a freshman basketball star, and cushion my fanny to sit comfortably on the bench. I had lost the opportunity to stay on the first string while we were learning about the rest of the world. Regrets? Not a bit. As I look back today, I have the same admonitions we expressed on the bow of the Cunard liner Berengaria for the young who must carry on.

CHAPTER

4.

Stanford Again

It is Stanford for both of us

Ted and I had just returned home to start our next semesters, Ted's first at Stanford. The qualities I seem to have manifested up to this time were:

1. To do the best I can everyday in a way that I am content within myself.

2. To not set professional goals as prods to achievement. Take each day one at a time, keeping the doors open to the future by all-around preparation for a lifetime's work that is within my potential. The goal of inner satisfaction is never lost.

Thus, a career in music and art were not a consideration. My tinkering talents and comfort with the common sense math of algebra and interest in the outside world were ready to be used. Was it not strange that practicing medicine had never really occurred to me?

Basketball

Like rugby in the destiny of Nelson Mandela, basketball was a major giveaway as to values already manifest that would guide me throughout my lifetime. They are not special, but they did not include having to win and in the process be sure others lose. At times, I may seem like a wimp. Let me say to others with like tendencies, "You are not a wimp either." In fact, you are quite the opposite. You don't have to throw a punch to be a man, as Bill O'Reilly suggests. You just have to duck as you grab the hand and make a friend. Let's see how this went over the next four years for this non-combative guy whose contest lay hidden within. Was it hard to hold back? Absolutely not. It was just plain natural. My first mentors, Mom and Dad, had taught me well.

The chance to play first string with Hank Luisetti was clearly gone. Coach John Bunn had utter faith in the team he had formed and rarely substituted, even when someone was clearly dogging it. This was never true for Hank, who gave of himself to the last whistle. So, I toughened my fanny and accepted my role as second stringer. Other fine players, feeling slighted, turned in their suits, but not Dick. It was my intent, and thus a joy, just to be on the

"JUMP BALL"
STANFORD vs. LONG ISLAND U.
MADISON SQUARE GARDEN
1938

court with this man five practice days a week, and at training table each night. I treasured the banter with this group of superb athletes. Did I have to win? I was winning every moment by my standards. I didn't make the travel team the first year, but did the second, as Hank demolished vaunted Long Island University for the second time and put our western cow college on the map more effectively than did a string of Nobel Prize Laureates. Just a few minutes of playing time against CCNY has been my treasured memory as I have milked the joy out of every moment, a habit ingrained for life.

An incident that occurred at the start of my second year is revealing to me as I look back. Because of my ability to swim butterfly as well as do the standard breast stroke, with two others we broke the Pacific Coast Medley Relay record. But swimming was just plain "no fun" for me. Practice laps were so alone and boring, and my swimming muscles, painfully acquired as my tight basketball muscles were untangled, left me with a discoordination that prevented me from swinging a golf club or tennis racquet effectively. That was too high a price, for golf with Dad and my brothers still had priority.

Swimming coach Nort Thornton asked Hank if I would make the team. Hank, to my surprise, said, "I don't think so." Nort then came to me to report this and to recruit me as a goalie on the water polo team.

The frog kick of the breast stroke allows a goalie to be pushed high in the net. "Nort," I said, "You have just made a mistake. I will make the basketball team." And I did, and did not swim again in my final year.

Of course I had to help win in any team play, whether basketball, rugby, or tennis doubles, but having to win in no way competed with playing a great game that brought the best out of my adversaries, as they often won, while I was at peace with myself.

My hernia vs. my basketball season

In February of my sophomore year, I noticed a little bulge in my right groin. I panicked, got in the car, and drove up to see Uncle Bert Meads about the problem. He didn't exactly laugh, but said, "It is just a hernia, and I can fix that." "Not now, please," was my rejoinder. We agreed to fix it in the summer, but I had to get by in the meantime.

Of course, a hernia sounds like something awful to a young kid. Uncle Bert said he would keep it a secret. I said I would do what I could not to get kicked off the team by Doc Northway, who seemed to know everything about his charges.

How would I get by with this? By then, I had appreciated that if you weren't self-conscious or looking embarrassed and in this way directing attention to yourself, your imperfections might go unnoticed. Just play it straight. I reasoned that a second supporter, or jock strap, pulled tightly into the groin as a truss would do the job. At the least, it deserved a try. As it turned out, I was not aware of the hernia at any time, even with intense play.

Each day in the dressing room, and in front of all my teammates, I put on two jockstraps, while looking directly at them. Can you believe it? No one ever noticed, let alone commented. I played out the season.

The lesson? If you don't point out your self-perceived deformities or shortcomings to others, you're likely to carry the day. It's all in the light of your eye.

The hernia repair was a cinch, as I would find out on making hundreds of these repairs in the young later on, but how different our

51

concepts were then as to aftercare. Although healthy and strong, I was kept in bed for ten days in the hospital. When told to get up, I fell flat on my face on the floor, so weak were my muscles and balance. Not the way to go. Once a surgeon, my rule would be to get patients on their feet almost immediately, no matter how serious the surgery. They didn't need to know my history and thus my reason to make such a demand.

There's a little more to the story. I was told to go home and rest. Are you kidding? I felt fine and believed I knew how not to strain my operative site. I got in the car and drove up to The Cedars in the mountains. The next day I went down the river a mile or so to the Big Pool to fish. I had the Contax camera on my back. I cast my line, slipped, and looked down about 50 feet to the pool, as a strong little tree went by untouched as I slid. Why untouched? A sudden jolt could undo the sutures. Better to go into the pool, camera and all, staying completely relaxed. It worked, and I climbed out and started home, anxious to start drying out the camera.

Half way up I met friends looking for me, a member of this rescue party with a past hernia repair leading the pack. We sped home together, I none the worse for wear. After all I had had a superior surgeon do the job. At dinner that evening, this member told me that he had to have a second repair, because he had driven his car too early. I reached down and all seemed well. I drove home unscathed. My hernia repair survived strenuous days on the basketball court and rugby field. Sure got my money's worth, Uncle Bert.

Fraternity life

Stanford life in that day centered on the fraternities and sororities. In them were the majority of movers and shakers. My House, Zeta Psi, stood by itself on the road leading to the residence of Ray Lyman Wilbur, Stanford's President. He was a towering personality within and without. As Secretary of the Interior under President Herbert Hoover, he had been able to provide protection to The Cedars, an enclave near Donner Pass in the Sierras. It had been owned by Mark Hopkins as part of the land grants of ten square miles of land for each mile of track, earned as the trancontinental railroad was cut through the mountains in 1868.

I suspect that Zeta Psi, if history notices it, will have a special place. It housed, in my time, five All American football players, two student body presidents, every other member a major sport letterman, and at least three Phi Beta Kappas, all in my class, and I was one of these. We were considered the campus "roughs." Our daily attire was jeans. We were in no way "High Society" and were in stark contrast to our major rivals, at least for coeds' affections, the Dekes. Their bow ties and tails routinely graced San Francisco soirees. Dr. Wilbur would wave to his "roughs" as he went home each day.

To me, what set Zeta Psi apart was that these boys were already men. Hazing and traumatic initiations ruled fraternities of the day. The Zeta Psi fraternity had no time for such trivia. I saw a paddle used just once, when a spoiled son of a Hollywood mogul was absent routinely from his Saturday housework, despite many warnings. The paddle had to be used, and only the smallest man in the House agreed to wield it. It worked, as it was supposed to on any immature boy.

Initiation was a chore for all. It amounted to sitting on a hard chair throughout a Saturday, enduring only the fierce halitosis of an older Zete close up as he told of the Zeta Psi history at length, yet this was the house that was termed "The Zoo" by others on The Row!

There were, of course, pranks as part of those carefree days before Pearl Harbor; the War would thin our numbers by at least three. Perhaps the most illustrious prank took place the night when Red Fay and Don Williams, anticipating a win for our Stanford team coached by Clark Shaughnessy, with hack saws weakened the new "impregnable" iron goal posts in Cal Berkeley's Memorial Stadium. After the win the next day, and with five Zetes on the team, the goal posts were felled as the "brothers" gave it a push.

On our return from the travels of 1936, Ted became a Zete and was dubbed "Polo," as I became "Marco." That fraternity nickname has followed me the rest of my life. "Hey, Marco!" tells me that a Zete buddy is hailing me, and warm memories flood.

As my four and a half years of college ended, a decision was demanded. I had followed my intent to keep all of the doors open. Boalt Hall School of Law in Berkeley had accepted my application. I had a scholarship waiting at MIT in Aeronautical Engineering, made possible by a wealthy MIT supporter, also Dad's dear friend. Business School was not an option, for it didn't exist. Harold Bacon, a mentor, had seen to it that I was admitted to Phi Beta Kappa. He had broken all the rules, for Engineering was not then an acceptable Humanities major. My guess is that I could easily have ended up at Boalt Hall, preparing for work in international law as I retained my desire to see more of the world and its people.

My greatest decision, obvious, but hidden from the start

Bill Hawkins, dear friend and Student Body President, and I were talking about our futures when I exclaimed, "Bill, I am so proud of you for your becoming a doctor." A few seconds passed. I said, "I am going to medical school, too." That was it. No hesitation. Why?

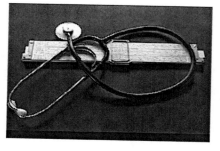

It was obvious that the years of experimenting and perhaps denying were over. My fears of the demands of dedication and confinement had to be overcome or perhaps, more to the point, accepted. Everything I had studied, in a roundabout way, was really preparation to meet a single end.

I had to believe that each day I would be doing something for someone and be assured of satisfying, tangible results. At the same time, accumulation of wealth was not my wish. I hoped that service as a doctor would be rewarded with an income sufficient to meet family needs yet to be defined.

A revealing Pre-med year at UC Berkeley

The die was instantly cast. The family tradition of not dallying over a decision prevailed. I had to spend a year in Pre-med, hoping the thought processes honed in Engineering would be an asset. They would be that, for sure, but in a way I did not imagine.

The year of Pre-med at Berkeley was an eye opener. It was the first time since high school that I became conscious of the Quick Memory minds. This time, though, the contest was for keeps. I had taken Biology in my freshman year at Stanford, but had not the time to do more than use what quick memory I had available to get by. My opening course in Embryology with Dr. Long, known as a dour martinet, left no doubt I was in for an intensive year. My Phi Beta Kappa key was just a memory as I kept it well out of sight and wondered what I had gotten into. When I heard the term epididymis, which would be a mainstay of my eventual specialty, urology, I had to look at my neighbor's lucid notes just to spell it. One thousand aspirants filled the lecture room. Nowhere was the intensity of competition more evident than in the lab, as students hid their findings in the microscope as though sharing was out of the question. It was the night before the final when I finally recognized what a somite (developing vertebra) was. I barely got through with a D as I relearned the prerequisite biology long forgotten, to then be amplified into embryology. This was a different world I was sampling.

My professor of Organic Chemistry was just as cold and suspicious. When I asked him for a little help, I was accused of buttering him up. All was not lost, though, for I found a human being in Dr. Aitken, who taught Advanced Biology. He was a born teacher and told me of his love to encourage the minds going into medicine. That was his calling, yet the powers that be required his next two years in narrow, isolated research.

Dr. Nafzigger, a member of The Cedars and the powerful University of California Professor of Neurosurgery, was pleased at my decision and started planning how to eventually have me as his resident. However,

I had another concern: my decision to be a doctor had, at the least, to have a happy beginning. The bookworms I had been exposed to at Berkeley left me cold. Familiar Stanford offered my best hope. Although I am sure my Pre-med grades didn't pass the test, my varied career there and a personal interview with perhaps the wisest man I have ever known, Stanford's Dean George Barnett, turned the tide. I would be Stanford's first engineer-doctor in a long time. My education in real life was just beginning.

My doors would now be open to internship and residency in a specialty I would eventually choose. I would be letting the cards fall where they may until then. Again, if I filled every day, the future would open wide.

CHAPTER

5.

Blue Beauty

Blue Beauty makes transition from engineer to doctor a pleasure

One of the books I loved most as a boy told the story of a black stallion known as Black Beauty. Thus, it was a natural for another story to really take place.

I had just decided to become a doctor, not an engineer after all. This change required I that add another year of education to cover Premed studies. It was least expensively achieved at UC Berkeley, just a few miles away from our home in Happy Valley. Wheels were a necessity for the first time. Somehow, I had sequestered $600 doing odd jobs at Stanford and during the winter vacation scrambling up stairs with Christmas loads for the Postal Service. Why not look at used car lots and make a good choice?

I started my search in 1939 by approaching the Buick used-car department in the premier agency in San Francisco. I was standing in the shop when a deep blue Buick Roadmaster convertible sedan rolled in. I assumed that it was there for repairs. Admiringly, I inquired as to its year and horsepower. The foreman said, "I am not sure. It's here just as a trade-in."

I asked, "What do you want for it?"

"$600."

"I'll take it!" I hastily wrote out the check, jumped in the seat,

and started the engine.

"But we haven't checked it out and serviced it."

"Just fine. I'll drive it out as is." I was taking no chances that someone else might see the gem I had discovered and slip away with it. Blue Beauty had black leather seats, the slickest and most comfortable I had ever seen, and the power that made just ordinary driving a ride in a chauffeured limousine.

It quickly became the convertible sedan of choice in Berkeley, always in place in the parking lot, ready to go as I lunched at the Zeta Psi fraternity house. Its chariot duties extended to being mobilized, with me as chauffeur, to make rounds at other fraternities—the Dekes, most often—as the parties wore down. Blue Beauty and I would pick up beautiful dates of incapacitated, somnolent Zete brothers, then to deliver the ladies to the safety of their sorority abodes. I guess my nickname, "The Sultan," was earned and well deserved; I was just a darned trustworthy guy as a driver and perhaps a father figure, but what else could one expect of a brother Zete from Stanford? And when it came time for the spring parade with its King and Queen, Blue Beauty was the chosen chariot, now "spoiled" by its garland of flowers.

Treasure Island in San Francisco Bay had just been created, and the 1939-1940 World's Fair would dedicate it. Many industries would be represented there and just as many entertainment venues. I was first attracted to Esther Williams and her Aquacade. They had advertised for swimmers proficient in freestyle and backstroke, and breaststrokers who also "fly." It was a natural for me, having been a member of Stanford's record-setting medley threesome. A buddy, a champion swimmer on the UC team, who possessed one of the most beautiful freestyle strokes I had ever seen, joined me. We two went to the Fairmont Hotel's inside pool for tryouts. As I remember, we were a little put off by the appearances of swimmers competing with us—these weren't college kids. They looked like older pros, probably mobilized from Hollywood itself or recruited from lifeguards on Southern California beaches. However, if ability was to be the determinant, neither of us felt threatened.

Blue Beauty

Several hours later, all of the swimmers lined up in the Civic Auditorium, there to be examined by the old master himself, tiny Billy Rose. He came down the line, looking up at these big specimens, accompanied by his secretary, tally board in hand. Mr. Rose, moving briskly, stopped directly in front of the two of us. My swimmer friend was also 6'3", and as handsome as they come. Billy looked at the two us as if surprised, perhaps, by unfamiliar faces. He turned to his secretary. "What about these two?" It took just a "no-no" twist of his head to ding us. Our summer careers in an exotic enterprise had ended.

Then I learned that Ford Motor Company was testing applicants as lecturers for their exhibit almost across the street from the Esther Williams water show. I don't recall how many of us appeared to be put through the traces of public speaking, but two of us were chosen. Morrie Chase, handsome, tall and spare, with a lively countenance and manner, and I were the lucky ones. I found myself the lead speaker, guiding visitors every thirty minutes through a delightful line of old carriages, some that had belonged to the legendary San Francisco Gold Rush era barons such as Charles Crocker and Leland Stanford. For once I found memorization not a chore, because these vehicles were real. Carriages and stories blended. I had the freedom to speak as the spirit directed. On many occasions, a listener would point out a juicy tidbit dating back to the days when they had seen these treasures roll by.

Morrie and I somehow acquired each other's talks, I guess just from listening to each other so many times as we followed along with the visitors, and we would improve both presentations. We were surely different in so many ways, but had in common the desire to do our jobs well, our senses of humor overlapping. Morrie was on his way to being a Catholic priest. He must have been a wonder, so well prepared at the altar of the Ford exhibit.

Blue Beauty, always ready to go, carried us workers back and forth each day to man the Ford exhibit on Treasure Island. We would direct her across the Bay Bridge, top down on these summer days, even as we pierced the morning fog, hair blowing in the sea breezes as we

59

anticipated another day doing a delightful job. We felt a little smug as we looked across the way to the Aquacade, feeling sorry for the poor souls mechanically paddling above and below the waves, not having time to blow noses on handkerchiefs as their physical resistance broke down.

Summer ended and it became time to start medical school at Stanford. The car gave me away. I was obviously the wealthy son of a wealthy father named Harvey Lyon, the man with the warehouse and the vans that said, "Let Lyon Guard Your Goods." They were wrong about the wealth, but I had it coming to me. Yet, explaining was not my style, and my buddies were happy to pile in, top always down, as we raced late for class. At times, the course took us off the roads and across weedy fields, but Blue Beauty absorbed the bumps without a whimper.

Pearl Harbor happened as we finished our first year on the Stanford campus. Our next years were spent in San Francisco. With the onset of real war, we had all become Navy or Army ensigns and GI's, and in uniform. I chose the Navy, having been already prepared by experiences with naval aviator Uncle Tom. He had been the Executive Officer of the Langley, our pioneering aircraft carrier—an old navy collier transformed by a deck that became a landing pad. I also envisioned having a berth with shower heads close by, no matter the battle. What an illusion that was, although in the Marine Corps showers would be provided when not in combat on the beach.

Blue Beauty had to be slowed to a walk, for gas rationing was severe. Horsepower was now used to attend classes, infrequent trips home across the Bay, and occasional dates. Gasoline was such a luxury that after graduation and my assignment to Boston, Blue Beauty had to be garaged in its "stall" in Hidden Valley. And then for a brief few days between my Boston internship and Marine induction at Parris Island in Virginia, we had a few runs together, old Blue just as sprightly as ever.

The Bombs at Hiroshima and Nagasaki ended the war. I was in the process of clambering up the rope ladder to the APA, attack personnel

60

transport, that would have taken us through murderous kamikazes and landed us on the beach of Kyushu, and had been given the sure reprieve of life.

At the Naval Supply Depot in Alameda after the war, I continued my life as a battalion surgeon. With gas rationing no longer, Blue Beauty would spring to life and we would smoothly "single-foot" together—skiing, dating, and just humming along under sunny California skies.

Blue Beauty deserved to have its own pasture after such noble service. This meant going into storage, placed on blocks, there to grow arthritic with rust while it waited to become a "classic" car, a designation quite unknown in those days. I could not allow this. My Chief Petty Officer fell in love with Blue, and so it became his.

We all have certain dogs, cats, or horses close to our hearts and with life expectancies far short of ours. Blue Beauty's lifetime could match ours, but only with continuous loving care. I go to automobile shows looking for her. Her lines would be unmistakable. When I do come upon a 1936 Buick Roadmaster Convertible Cabriolet, it is my Blue Beauty every time. I imagine Blue Beauty saying, "Hi there. Those days we can't forget."

6.

Medical School

I become a Stanford medical student

From the first day, my classmates seemed so accomplished as they told me of their activities, their records giving them an aura that was impressive. However, we would see; I understood hard work. My engineer's mind could recognize and unearth, then retain, facts and principles that would hang together. Thus, Anatomy, Neurology, and Physiology were joys as I traced and imbedded tracks, switches, and stations in my Process Mind for instant recall when a problem presented. The Quick Memorizers were neatly filing them in separate folders.

All in all, my starting grades were mediocre as I committed to memory Bacteriology and Chemistry. When we moved to Stanford Hospital for our clinical years, I began to feel the confidence in Process Thinking as the art of a meaningful history was mastered while hands probed for telltale signs, and laboratory results were factored in. I was at home, and, for the first time, fell under the spell of the wisdom in which I was being immersed.

Thomas Addis, who would be my Stanford mentor in my education about the kidney, reminded me of the High Lama in *Lost Horizon*, as his foresight would not limit diagnostic powers just to initial treatment. With his hands in the front pockets of his long white smock, we spent delightful hours together, my ears taking in every word. As a mentor, he was top of the line. He was concerned about the long haul and was almost the first to what we now call "follow up" his patients. Dad had schooled me well in this rule for constructive living. Others had "impressions." Not Dr. Addis. He kept meticulous records, setting a standard I would easily follow. He had reduced tests to a simplicity that allowed me, now his student assistant, to within a half hour of taking my patient's history, complete the work up, and establish the diagnosis. He left no doubt that diagnosis follows facts, a dictum Dr. Frank Hinman would later affirm. Dr. Addis's creatinine clearance test is the standard even today, although the joy of promptly making a diagnosis and starting treatment has been lost, as these tests must go now to the hospital lab, impersonal, and delaying treatment.

Yet something else set him apart: the completely honest scientist—his animal studies proved that—established that, contrary to current practice, a high protein diet was not necessary to make up for the protein lost in the urine of kidney disease. His low-protein diet is still a staple, although others claim credit. Did he take notice? I think not. His humility may have been a hindrance to fame, but he knew that he was being *effective*. I suspect I am one of his products, for that lesson was not lost on me.

Our San Francisco boarding house

After eighteen months of training in the basic sciences on the Stanford campus, we moved to San Francisco for our clinical years. My years in San Francisco were not unlike the story of the students at Johns Hopkins who came to life in a boarding house run by Susie Schlegal. Eight of us would sit around a table, white tablecloth always, at a sumptuous dinner each weeknight. Our two elderly hostesses and cooks had raised families, come to the big city, rented this old Victorian, and we showed up. The banter would start, and look out! All of us had had our fill of fraternity life, but the give and take of happy banter was ingrained. Sherm Mellinkoff, later to be dean of the medical school at UCLA, Brandy Bassett, who would become a urologist in Oakland, and John Peal, headed for Professor of Pediatrics at UC, would be the aggressors as the rest of us, especially Jim Wilson and I, would try to keep up with the smooth talkers. We were all in uniform, tuitions now paid for, preparing for active duty after internships, but the war was still far away at the time.

In teaching-ward rounds, I was known, all in good humor, as "the guy who asked the dumb questions." My Process Mind had to understand to remember, but there turned out to be a positive side. Joe Oyster and I were walking away from a makeshift graduation ceremony when I said, "Joe, it has been so much fun to be with you, even though you are the number one man in the class. Your photographic memory has produced so many laughs when you tie up our hopeless psychiatry professor by repeating word for word the gobbledygook paragraph you read to us the night before."

"Dick, let me explain. It isn't what you think. My photographic mind has been a terrible load to bear. I have never learned to think. I will be a good doctor. You will be something else." At the time, I didn't get the point. Perhaps he was prophetic. I came to realize that possibly my plodding and straining to understand could stand me in good stead after all.

I "breakaway" at Stanford, as well as being a medical student

When I returned to Stanford, my Pre-med experience at Berkeley had allowed me to be introduced to rugby, and "breakaway" was a natural fit for a basketball player. Rugby is a non-letter sport, and any student, graduate or not, could play. I played second string at UC Berkeley and somehow scored the six points for a win against my Alma Mater.

Back at Stanford in medical school, I went out for the team. A fine breakaway and good friend, Ted Cole was injured. I was given his first string job and stayed there. I played with the football greats, All-American mountainous fullback Norm Standlee, scatback and All-American Pete  Kemetovick, and Frankie Albert, All-American quarterback. As safety, he was still phenomenal, demonstrating the same talents in rugby as on the football field. We won all of our games, but I will never forget USC, whose footballers played rugby, too, and like the blundering tough guys they were. Their attitude was "to heck with the rules" and "even if we could understand them, we'll just roll over you." That worked for the first half. I and the other Stanfords wondered if we could take the clumsy beating for another half. Well, they were more exhausted than we, and our knowledge of the game allowed us to roll easily over them, making 21 points in the second half.

In medical school, which continued in the clinics in San Francisco, I again played rugby for the Olympic Club in San Francisco. In our game with Cal, I found myself in the lineout battling a guy who was younger, bigger, and much stronger. I realized he was using hands and elbows on me where really just moving hips is enough, as in basketball, to keep the other guy off balance. At any rate, I finally said to him, "You're playing dirty and I don't like it." California coach Doc Hudson benched him for his actions.

Three years later, as I ran the urology clinic as resident, who did I see as my student, now in a white coat, but Peterson. I asked him if he remembered me, because I remembered him as the dirtiest rugby player I knew. He did. I asked him why he didn't take a swing at me that day.

"Well," said Peterson, "I am not taking a swing at the Pacific Coast Boxing Champion." Smart boy! But what he didn't know, and still doesn't, is that in my class at Stanford there was another Dick Lyon. He was a Deke, who at 110 pounds, was the Flyweight Pacific Coast Conference champion.

So, that was a positive fallout from the name Lyon. It balanced Dad's experience with his name that cost him a scholarship for me to get through college. On the other hand, I knew honesty is the best policy, but in this case I turned honesty a little on its head, figuring Peterson was content with his excellent judgment. Why spoil that?

Next to basketball, rugby is the queen of competitive contact team sports, because it is played without protection. There is no blocking or direct tackling, save going for the ball. It is rough, but the kind of roughness enjoyable to one such as myself whose contact is rarely direct, but slanting as you throw each other off balance. Some of the most beautiful open field running is possible. I remember the Irish playing Cal. After a scoreless and gentlemanly first half, Dr. Kyle, physician and their All-Irish hero, simply took the ball on three runs the length of the field, scoring each time as he left his defenders astonished, in broken-field runs that put our football abilities to shame, and all in the good spirit that typified the sport. Nelson Mandela will attest to all of this.

Olympic club hypoxia—a learning process

One afternoon it was so quiet at the Olympic Club that I decided to take a swim all by myself. I had been given a scholarship there to play basketball and rugby. No one was around, and the Olympic-sized pool, 50 yards long, needed some action. I had thoroughly enjoyed my basic Physiology class in medical school and often wondered about the process of rebreathing, the intent being to empty the lungs of carbon dioxide (CO_2), which is the actual stimulus to take a breath, rather than just a shortage of oxygen. I knew that pearl divers did this, so why not give it a try?

So, rebreathing aggressively, I dove in. It was my intent to go as far as possible without surfacing, my breast stroke being so effective. I swam the first fifty yards and made the turn starting back. At 75 yards, I felt as though I could go on forever, still not needing to take a breath. This was at least twice as far and twice as long underwater as I had ever experienced. Then common sense chimed in. I realized that something was wrong. It was almost a panic. I came to the surface, not a bit out of breath, but alive! If I hadn't come up, who knows? Sometime later, I read of a young man on the same jaunt found dead at the bottom of the pool, and that possibility was quite real that day for me, as I had experienced a kind of fatal euphoria. I am told that such is not uncommon among deep sea divers.

The lesson? Keep thinking, no matter the momentary happiness, in anything you do. I don't recall my teacher ever mentioning if hypoxia (low oxygen) would kick in in time to save one's life. Apparently not, but I was allowed to keep filling my responsibilities ahead whatever they might be. A very, very close call!

Learning clinical medicine and becoming real doctors

We sixty students were a congenial bunch. We appreciated the dedication of our teachers. They were overworked leaders in their fields, teaching on top of immense practice loads, as they covered for their overseas fellows. After graduation, when I would go on with my surgical training in the East, I would recognize the remarkable wisdom I had received from these giants, for later in Boston I found myself fully prepared, often better than those trained at Harvard and other prestigious schools.

A good laugh was always at hand. One example is the day on rounds that Leo Eloesser, Viennese and world famous, was working over my group of six. All five feet of him would stare up at the tallest, me in this case. He asked me what I knew about synovial fluid (the lubricant of the joints). Completely unprepared for anything about orthopedics, I said, "Sir, I know it looks like water." He then turned to Joe Oyster, not much taller than he, and accepted as the top student in our class, saying, in jest, "Professor, what can you tell me?" We stood open mouthed as Joe detailed for minutes about everything from salt content to enzymes. Where had we been all of the time? Dr. Eloesser replied, "Professor, I believe you are making that up." "Yes, Sir," was Joe's response. The good doctor smiled, then walked out to drive to his office in his massive red Cadillac convertible, top down, with a Pekinese Poodle resting in each corner. Can't beat that.

One day at lunch after urology clinic, Frank Norman informed us, "I just met a crazy resident. I was trying to make him feel at home, for he had obviously recently come here. His Nordic accent was obvious. I told him how much I enjoyed a most beautiful Swedish actress I had just seen at the movie last night. Her name is Ingrid Bergman. Guess what this guy said? 'Yes, I know. She is my vife.'" Of course. Now we knew that our resident was her husband, Peter Lindstrom. We all went to the movies that night.

I open a door and look inside

So, where was I in my development as a physician-to-be? First, I was clearly on course, hands on each day as I learned about and at times even added to the patients' care. My Process Mind was proving adequate for the job, though I seemed to learn differently from my fellows. It was still one day at a time as I searched for signposts to an internship with the most promise. I had decided, for sure, that I wished to be exposed to various points of view. I believed that this would be best served by going to the medical Holy City, said to be Boston. That would surely keep the doors open and perhaps open new doors, for the internship was just a necessary stepping stone. I recognized from the start that my tinkering tendency would only be satisfied in a field of surgery. However, I also believed that a thorough grounding in internal medicine and its revelations as to body physiology should be my foundation before wielding the knife.

The Thorndyke Institute at Boston City Hospital was the prize internship for me. I applied and took the exam, but didn't make the grade. Apparently I had a knowledge deficiency, for I knew nothing about vascular disease, most prominently that of thrombophlebitis. Later on, I was to learn that this complication, usually following surgery or with prolonged illness, was endemic in the hot and cold East and almost never seen in our even, western climate. No wonder eastern students were primed with answers about it.

"Fate" takes a hand, I think

Fate now stepped in as Bob Evans, our hematologist, somehow learned of my disappointment. Why hadn't I told him of my hopes, even though I was a do-it-on-my-own guy? Big mistake, and one that I would now learn from. That evening on the phone was William B. Castle, a great man, the father of the cure of pernicious anemia, and the boss at Thorndyke. He said I was now the first alternate, and he would keep in touch. Guess I had gotten a good grade in hematology.

Then there was silence. The Navy began to breathe down my back and was ready to put me on active duty if a civilian internship was not acquired. Then, just in time, Dr. Castle called back, saying, "Would you accept a surgical internship? All of our applicants are making it." My answer was that I would do anything to get to Boston. The 4th Surgical Service would be the bottom of the heap, for it was the only one having no medical school affiliation. So what? I would make it work.

It may seem odd, but I had no qualms about not winning the top-of-the-line job. Why? Because, like some doggerel I can't quite remember, "If it ain't good, I'll make it so." I was learning that life's decisions are made in the light of one's eye. What others saw was not important. What was in my eye was all that counted. In retrospect, what my eye saw in 4th Surgical would make it perhaps the most valuable, and thus treasured, training experience of my lifetime.

CHAPTER

7.

Boston Internship

An internship for a lifetime

What were those nine months really like? My room was tiny, and I made my own bed. Food was abundant and free for house officers. It was at hasty meal times that we learned about each other. $25 a month was our pay, and we had to supply our own sneakers, typically worn through every three months, as we walked, more often ran, through the miles of connecting tunnels. Cases would be seen at Admitting and parceled out in an orderly fashion to six surgical services, each manned by nine house officers. Operating room procedures would be monitored by experienced and, occasionally, famous surgeons in private practice. There was only one anesthesiologist; the others were away at war. Peter Saunders made each of us, interns particularly, proficient with spinal anaesthesia, and the new intravenous Pentothal. We rotated through the specialties—neurosurgery, general surgery, orthopedics, and urology. Although we were encouraged to go it on our own, never was supervision not acting. I averaged 4-1/2 hours of sleep a night. This included our biweekly Saturday afternoon and Sunday days off. I learned to catnap day and night, and I can't remember ever being tired. I treasured the middle-of-the-night challenges, because that seemed to be when everything was happening, and I would learn the most.

There was something else for me—I would get my internal medicine education as I squeezed out time to go to medical rounds. Dr. Castle often presented the puzzles inherent in exotic cases. Could I have ever imagined seeing three patients at one time with Addison's Disease (adrenal gland failure) treated with expensive hormones? Cortisone was then at least 15 years away.

A treasured memory is the day on ward rounds when I was kibitzing the 50-student third-year class from Harvard. Dr. Castle had just examined a post-surgical patient with markedly distended abdomen and asked for a diagnosis. None scored. He saw me in back in my ragged surgical whites. Knowing me to be a surgical intern, he said, "Dr. Lyon, any ideas?"

"Sir, I believe it is a case of acute gastric dilation."

"Thank you Dr. Lyon. Your Stanford training has served you well."

Just as Hank scored against Long Island University in Madison Square Garden, so did I score as Stanford demolished Harvard that day. What Dr. Castle did not know was that Fritz Reichert, our Stanford neurosurgeon, had harped on this problem day after day, for he had seen a death when cardiac arrest had occurred, apparently triggered by unrecognized stomach distension. Thank you Dr. Reichert. The height of my medical education was reached by listening to, and then questioning, my elders— a habit that has followed me to this day.

Busiest day of my life

My first day on the job in orthopedics introduced me to the intensity of responsibilities to follow. I was given 30 patients. With each new patient, five or six a day, it was my responsibility to write the patient's history and record my physical findings, as well as examine the urine and test the blood, and do a spinal tap when inebriation was suspected. In that day, all intravenous fluids were administered by interns and residents. My day was a full one. Doctors are roundly criticized for their atrocious handwriting. I suspect I am a serious offender. Let me explain why. My high school writing teacher, Mrs. Beebe, directed that my handwriting meet the standards for legibility and appearance. Engineering trained my printing ability to the point I could print as fast as I could write longhand. My printed notes were passed around in medical school, so legible were they. Then, what happened?

The writing responsibilities and the time demands at City Hospital forced me to write as fast as possible. I found myself writing a hybrid of writing and printing that dogs me to this day, but the nurses learned to interpret it, and the work was done. In a way, it turned out to be a useful conspiracy between head nurses and this doctor. Miss Havis, the epitome of the ideal head nurse, at Berkeley's Alta Bates Hospital one day confided in me that only she could interpret my handwritten orders. She further admitted that top surgeon Dexter Richards and top internist Gale Whiting had the same defect. I was in great company. The payoff for her was that she could maintain tight control of her staff, as they checked with her when orders seemed unreadable. The same applied to pharmacists throughout the Bay area. They new instantly if the prescription they would fill was valid.

My one-month orthopedic rotation was a joy. Tinkering tendencies, combined with engineering concepts that required a three-dimensional grasp of the problem, made it possible for me to innovate from day one. A patient was admitted with a shattered elbow that would normally require anaesthesia and possibly open surgical reduction. Instead, with cables, pulleys, and eye-screws purchased at the hardware store nearby, his arm was literally hung up, as day by day I molded the fragments into place. A first hip nailing was scheduled. Who got the job? This engineer, who then, in a tiny hot room equipped with a portable X-ray unit, drilled into bone and inserted the pin, and it worked! A fractured tibia seen in the emergency room gave me a chance to use the just acquired intravenous Sodium Pentothal for the few minutes it took to drill a hole in the bone, place a rod called a Steinman Pin, and then seal it all in plaster and send him home.

From the start, I was wonderfully at home in Boston City Hospital, where my boss watched every step and approved. He suggested that I approach Dr. Green at Peter Bent Hospital, the father of pediatric orthopedics, as to a residency with him. Even then it was becoming clear that my heart would be with the kids. He offered me the residency; residents were in short supply due to the war. I didn't get the chance, however, for someone in Washington made the decision to send me to the front. That terminated at least one possibility for my future professional life.

I had toyed with the idea of returning to San Francisco and starting a neurosurgical residency with Dr. Nafzigger, if he would still have me. Neurosurgery was really still in its infancy, but something was wrong. We would operate, remove a brain tumor, and produce a "vegetable." I wouldn't be content, no matter the stimulus of intricate surgery. Another possible specialty bit the dust. As luck would have it, my second rotation was with a famous man, Dr. Donald Munroe, who, also a tinkerer, had created a tool to rehabilitate bladders, known as the Monroe Drainage (eventually I would use it as a urologist). Urology problems were not stimulating, and this specialty, too, at that time did not appeal to me. Thus it was the surgical internship that taught me the most lessons. Two incidents in the hands of my mentors are illustrative.

My surgical mentors

Knute Browder was our most attentive mentor. He was grizzled and gruff and noted for fast surgeries. For instance, a gall bladder removal in 15 minutes was his rule. I asked him why so fast? He told me that with the doctor shortage, he would have to do up to 12 cases a day. And then there was the matter of blood loss. It's hard to believe, but surgical transfusions were just coming into use, spurred by experience on the battlefields. The faster the surgery, he had found, the less the blood loss. It all made sense.

One day I admitted a patient with a "hot" appendix, and Dr. Moles, my erratic resident, would do the case, Dr. Browder supervising. As Bob Moles started to make the long mid-line incision demanded in all Boston City Hospital cases where the initial diagnosis was often in doubt, Knute grabbed Moles's hand and said, "Let's do it right, through a McBurney." This is a tiny incision over the appendix and favored by most old-timers. The incision was made, and Moles's probing finger searched for the appendix. No luck. Knute's finger went in and instantly up popped a long black appendix, we supposed at the point of rupture. Not so. As Dr. Moles reached for a clamp to remove the organ, Knute, instead, poked it back into the hole. Moles tried again, and again Knute had to pop up the gangrenous organ. Again Moles asked for the clamp. Again Knute said, "Not so fast. Try again," as the frightening organ was returned to its bed. Moles, by now sweating profusely, this time flipped up the appendix. It was removed, the patient none the worse for wear. What I was seeing was the massive wisdom of experience that told Knute Browder that there was still a ways to go before rupture, and Dr. Moles learned a valuable lesson.

A second mentor was Dr. Morrison. He was quite different from Dr. Browder. He was also in his sixties, handsome, tall, reserved and just as experienced. At midnight I admitted a man in his seventies with all of the classic telltale signs of an acute appendicitis. Classically, pain had started at the umbilicus and then moved into the right lower quadrant. That area was exquisitely tender.

Dr. Morrison came right in after, I am sure, a busy day. These mentors were dedicated, very special people. When he arrived, something had changed. The tenderness was gone! I was embarrassed and started to call the operating room to cancel the case. Dr. Morrison thought otherwise. "Dick, let's go."

At surgery I removed a reddish-black, swollen, "hot" appendix. How had I messed up? My lesson followed. Dr. Morrison said that in the elderly and occasionally in childhood, the tissue reaction would be a rapid accumulation of fluid, or transudate, that would act as a poultice, and for a little while it would mask the problem. How lucky could I be, for this warning was not in the books, and this was only one day of lessons at Boston City Hospital!

Learning could have its humorous side, too. On my first day on as a surgeon on 4 Surgical, Dr. Moles told me to admit a patient for Dr. Browder and get her ready for surgery. This lady gave me a history of recurrent flank pain. She was to have her kidney stuck in place. Nephropexy, or fixing the kidney so as to no longer drop, was a procedure not yet in my learning curve. Physical exam revealed nothing abnormal. I was to have another interesting learning experience ahead, I feared.

On ward rounds that afternoon, Dr. Moles read my report and said, "Dick, please examine her abdomen again." Wow! There was a round mobile mass in the right lower quadrant. It felt like a kidney, and I had missed it. Better go back to school was my first reaction. Embarrassed? You bet.

As we turned to leave the room, Dr. Moles said, "Mrs. Jones, you can put your kidney back now." With a twist and a turn, she reached down and with one motion, popped the kidney back into place in her side. I had been "had"—not knowing then that I would see my share of these in a urological practice not then considered a possibility.

My internship had slipped rapidly by. I had to go to war as a Navy Junior Lieutenant. At Newport, after a few lazy days of tennis, I was ordered to report to the Admiral. He looked as if he had bad news. From the Navy standpoint, he did. "Dr. Lyon, you are assigned to the Marines and will report immediately to Parris Island for training."

Surprised, I found myself smiling and saying, "That's great. I never considered being a Marine, but it suits me fine." I was thinking that there would be no cushy quarters and hot showers, but I couldn't remember anything I had enjoyed more than beating the rigors as a Boy Scout in camp. The Admiral shook his head.

CHAPTER
8.
I Become a Marine

A Marine is on his way.

With my entry into the Marine Corps came the next surprise. Instead of getting into the rigorous training I had expected and was a little anxious about, twenty-five other medical recruits and I were gathered around a table to receive some news. Half of us would be on our way west immediately, still fresh and untrained, to fill spots as Battalion Surgeons making ready for the next invasion.

The question: "Is there any reason anyone of you are not ready to go?"

"Is he kidding?" I whispered to Roland French, also from 4 Surgical. It wasn't a matter of being ready; it surely had to be, "Get Going!" The officer went around the table. There were more than a few that had such nebulous answers as to be funny, such as, "I need to take my wife home," and the like. I turned to Roland and whispered, "Is this guy serious? We're at war, aren't we?"

My answer was, "Sir, I can't think of a single reason not to go," believing this was all a show.

Roland and I were chosen with a few others. I went to the PX (post exchange) and outfitted myself in the real thing, a Marine uniform. Then I went to the dispatcher, who inquired, "How would you like to go?"

I replied, "Do you have a wagon train available?"

He laughed and said, "No, but would you like to take a route to, say, see a girlfriend?"

"Good idea. I'll go by way of New York." I did just that, stayed overnight, then landed in Pendleton, California, the next day.

That was when the fooling around stopped. I was promptly assigned to the 4th Marine Division training on the Hawaiian island of Maui. Hours later, I was on my way on an APA (Attack Personnel Transport) to the First Battalion, 24th Regiment, 4th Marine Division FMF (Fleet Marine Force), there to meet my new boss, Dr. Dick Porter, and be his assistant in the invasion moments away.

We Marines go west to something

Things didn't go the way I expected it would or should. We rendezvoused in Pearl Harbor, sitting immobile for three weeks as I watched the erosion of physical conditioning of our men. Daily tennis at the Officers' Club seemed like a dream, so I made the most of it. Finally, we steamed away to the west. Our destination, we were told, was a tiny island, Iwo Jima, well fortified and manned by seasoned troops. My comrades had been in three previous invasions, so I believed that I, the neophyte, was in the best hands possible. This proved to be so.

We sailed out as a convoy in our APA, 5,000 Marines and their explosives and vehicles. The nights were clear and the skies star-filled. When others were at the poker table or reading, I would wend my way through the dark, banging my head on bulkheads, to reach the foredeck. I would stand there looking up, identifying constellations I had just mentally photographed from my small star book. Going to and coming from Iwo Jima, I learned to identify 65 constellations and all of the navigational stars. My last exploit was to master the navigation forms, so that with a sextant I could pilot our APA, or a lifeboat at worst. One evening on the way back, I asked the navigation officer to show me how he did things. He took out a star book. I said, "Can't you identify the stars without that?" The officer, a dentist by trade, looked surprised, causing me to say, "I'm sure glad we are in the middle of a convoy."

Iwo Jima

We anchored in the company of thousands of ships of every kind.

Destroyers, cruisers, and battleships were shelling the island, as they had been doing for weeks. The first waves of Marines had reached the beach. Our turn to disembark and jump into landing craft occurred about 2:00 p.m. Our corpsmen were scattered into many LCVPs (landing craft) in order to make unlikely the loss of our whole unit from a single, direct hit. All headed for the beach, reaching it as darkness came on. All I remember is standing on sand at the water's edge in the midst of landing craft and looking for someone familiar. The beached ships were trying to deliver their goods as mortar blasts chipped away, the island's defenders having perfected their aim on the beaches. The death toll was immense, for our positions could be anticipated by the enemy, and easily zeroed in.

Coming out of nowhere, our executive officer, Buck Schecter, grabbed me and yelled, "Doc, let's get out of here. Follow me!" We scrambled up over the dunes to the vicinity of our battalion, each of us digging a foxhole with our small shovels, in which to hunker down for the night. No Spam or C-rations for the moment. The sky was alive with bright, whistling shells, thundering as they hit the sand and its occupants. That is all I can remember, except that a young Marine, afraid to the point of tears, lay in my arms throughout the night.

Strangely, I wasn't afraid. I was fascinated. Perhaps it was my acceptance of whatever might come as I devoted every moment to doing my job. I worked with our corpsmen, who didn't need to be told what to do. My Boy Scout first aid training served me well. The designation, Battalion Surgeon, was impressive, but in fact it was first aid all of the way.

With our combat platoons out in front, we support platoons worked our way northward up the beach just below the airfield. It was foxhole to foxhole. The engineer in this doc manifested when, time and time again, we would spot mortar shells, like speeding birds, coming our way. I placed sticks upright in such a way that I could, by triangulation, recognize those coming at us, though without knowing their eventual points of impact. They could be in front or behind, so that with a threatening sighting, I moved the medical unit one way or another and out of the line of fire. After six days, we reached the quarry that would be our home until our 26th day, when the island was finally secured and we departed.

Our medical unit and its docs, Dick Porter and I, were fortunate to have very likely the lowest casualty rate on the island. I think we were just plain lucky. Also, Big Dick Porter, all of 6'5," and most of the corpsman were seasoned veterans of three previous landings in the Marshall Islands' invasions. They knew their business and rules for survival, not the least of which was, "If someone calls for help, call for rifle cover, because the enemy marksman will be zeroed in on his hit and waiting for you."
Our only mortality occurred just that way. We lost one of our prized new corpsman, who had planned to go to medical school.

One of the challenges about which I became particularly sensitive was the matter of so-called "battle fatigues." These youngsters were being sent to the hospital ships to be forever tagged with guilt. Early on, I recognized that these episodes of terror were short and reversible. It was understandable that these Marines had to be evacuated so as not to put their platoons at risk. I took the responsibility of heavily sedating each boy with sleeping pills—really knocked him out—and letting him sleep for 12 hours or so. On awakening, calmed, he would talk with me. From that point on, almost every likely "battle fatigue" went back to his platoon, some becoming heroes, for all I know. The fallout was that, as we prepared for the next invasion where I would be boss, I pilfered a case of Sodium Pentothal from the regiment stores. I would then have the means to be truly effective. My Boston City Hospital experience with this new wonder drug was paying off. I was also becoming aware of the building blocks each day that experience provides, as once lined up, they can do wonderful things, although at the time of creating the blocks, they were just incidents.

In strife like this, humor is sidelined, for there isn't much humor to tap into in war. But there must be. For instance, we were told not to take cameras into combat. I understood this rule for, although my camera was my log, I had no desire either to have a camera eye recording the trauma I would see, or even to think about anything that would take my mind off my job, if just for an instant. However, it did occur to me that as we completed our mission, there might be a time when photos of our men might be worthwhile. Therefore, I placed my prized Contax camera in the safest place I could think of, the Exec's desk, hoping it might come ashore at a quiet time. On Day 20 or so, it was in direct view, 25 yards from the beach, when a mortar shell made a direct hit. I can still see the craft and its contents bubbling slowly as it descended to the bottom. I have to smile, though, for all that was lost could be replaced, and the boat master swam safely to shore.

This led me again to be the tinkerer. I recalled the original Eastman box camera with its single exposure shutter and no lens. Why not make a similar pinhole camera? I scrounged a roll of film, probably from a Marine cameraman, located a small box; made my pinhole, and took a dozen shots. This camera and its photos would today be in a museum, but that was not to be. Again, I tried to find the safest place for my treasure. It ended up in the stores on my medically-loaded Jeep, to be transported in the hold of our return ship. I still had a lot to learn. My Jeep was empty when we recovered it on Maui. My Marine buddies had a good laugh. Didn't I know that anytime there were goodies not locked up securely, especially coming home from combat, the swabbies would steal us blind, and then sell to starry-eyed recruits, even our C-ration utensils, as captured Japanese souvenirs?

The battle won, we go back to Maui and pick up the pieces

The return to Pearl Harbor was a time to enjoy good meals and a shower or two, to complete the solemn duty of writing to the families of our lost comrades, and to make recommendations for honors to be awarded for heroism.

Heroism is usually not obvious. It occurred quietly and unheralded many times each day on Iwo Jima. My experience with Corpsman Flores serves as an example. We lost one of our finest men in the sniping just described. I had a problem—either to send Danny Danhauer, a green corpsman without front-line platoon

experience—or to ask corpsman Flores, battle-wise after three invasions and known to all the platoons, to fill in as this battle was ending. His job was done. His war tour would be over and he was scheduled to be on his way to the mainland as soon as we left the island.

Flores said, "I'll go," picked up his carbine and disappeared over the brim of the hill into the valley of possible death. This was to me the ultimate bravery, based on the love that permeated our team of Navy Marines.

I requested that he be awarded the Silver Star. I had been warned that officers always got the benefit of the doubt, but not the enlisted men, so I had better ask for the higher honor. Flores received the Bronze Star. I don't think he ever understood why, surprised to receive any award at all. He was just doing his duty. What a privilege to be a Marine and a Navy man to boot!

Brother Bruce "missing in action"

I can never forget my mail the day we anchored in Honolulu. The last letter from Mom and Dad said Bruce was "missing in action." Quite by myself on the bow, I cried and cried and cried. Why such grief when he was "just missing in action," and there was still hope that his chute had carried him to safety? It had been twenty days, and there was still no word. I knew that a Lyon brother, no matter the circumstances, would have figured out some way to let Mom and Dad know that he was all right.

As the pilot of his B24 on his 32nd mission, and with a new crew returning from a successful raid, a defective bomb in his own bombbay,

82

or one dropped from a returning plane above, took the lives of all but three. Here surfaced another personal quality: Despite two different stories from a crew member and the doctor in his squadron, I took no joy in assessing blame; this would be a lifelong principle, for to me it was

only this day and the day ahead that could make a difference. So, get on with it, adjust, regroup, and move ahead. Move ahead? Bruce was gone. How would I respond? I would take on his mission and work harder than ever. Could I do the work of two? Absolutely. Our rules for living were the same. Joys and pain I would share. His Purple Heart graces this computer. Do I still grieve? Of course, and he has been a vital, driving part of anything I might have achieved.

We rest and then prepare again on Maui

On Maui the remnants of our regiment returned to tents, mess halls, and many days of just lolling about as we regrouped. Our Makawao base, on the west side of Mount Haleakala, was the spot on the island noted only for its rainfall. The Army had abandoned it as unlivable. What better place to toughen up a Marine? A day off would find us traveling by Jeep about two miles to the south, where abruptly the sheet of rain ended and sun bathed everything, so there were compensations.

Big Dick Porter had earned a battle-free berth after four invasions. I was now nominally the boss, but my Navy chiefs made everything go. I learned from Martin Middlewood and his men every day. Because the doc didn't have to march and struggle through the boondocks, I found myself organizing basketball teams for officers and enlisted men. A quartette with me as its tenor, good ear for harmony but a lousy squeaky voice, made us a fixture at the General's parties. What great food! I also played the accordion at officers' gatherings, as singing seemed to diminish inebriation. My new assistant, Doc Owen, was also trained in surgery. He would go on to an illustrious career in Seattle, but then was just as green as I had been four months earlier.

Before leaving the mainland, I had ordered every medical and surgical journal I could think of, to keep my mind active and up to date, thus we had our own medical library and the journals showed up, to the point that I that received the Mayo Clinic Bulletin on Day 15 on Iwo Jima. We two docs were swimmers in college, so on days off-duty, we drove to Maui's wild west coast, and with fins rode the surf. It sounds like it was all fun for the moment, and I guess it was. We didn't dwell on what lay ahead or make plans for the future. We knew they would be made for us soon enough.

Again, there were humorous happenings. Our battalion team won all of its games, as I coached the "uncoachables." It came down to the Maui championship, with the winner to go to Honolulu for the Pacific Theater Championship finals. We were a fast-breaking bunch. Our opponents were led by Indiana All-American guard Andy Phillips. They were deliberate stop-and-shoot artists. Col. Banks, our boss, ordered me to win. He had a bundle at risk.

Our first fast-break play landed Captain Joe Swoyer against the wall after a lay-up. Then mayhem broke loose. It suddenly dawned on us that the floor was hopelessly slippery, having been waxed for a dance the night before. Or did Andy and his Heavy Weapons battalion outsmart us and become wax-masters? Andy, laughing at me all the way, won the game and then the championship. Their joy, however, would be short lived, for it was just a few weeks later that we received our orders to prepare for our next invasion—the mainland of Japan. The chips were down.

I had given a great deal of thought to what we would face. My Japan travels had prepared me well to judge our enemy. They would be implacable, the peasants as well as the soldiers. The Bushido Samurai spirit of centuries would be manifest as death was the choice: to surrender was to be a coward, also punishable by death. Kamikazes would be our first barrier, striking us at sea as we would move sluggishly. Our APAs carried 5,000 Marines each, their vehicles and munitions below, veritable bombs in themselves. 10,000 kamikazes, dedicated to dying, meant that if only 1,000 survived our shellfire, that 1,000 would take a least 500,000 American lives, these the cream of the crop. Britain had taken the same beating, and its loss of the best and the brightest is manifest today in the indecision that followed.

This would be just the beginning. My First Battalion, 24th Regiment, would be the first wave on the lower island, Kyushu. I could only imagine the bloody encounters that would immediately ensue as we would fight our way, not only against soldiers, but also women and children armed with bats and perhaps knives. Our troops would have to be protected by undefendable bombing, often carpet-bombing. The devastation would be complete. Japan's loveliest cities, most filled with ancient treasures, would perish. Cities such as Kyoto and Nara, with their irreplaceable temples and gardens, would be turned to ashes. Our world would be forever maimed. Bombs would take hundreds of thousands, perhaps millions of Japanese lives. And yet there were still, in our halls of power at home, voices calling for restraint and discussion. Didn't they know anything about a Bushido culture, that free of any outside influence, was still in place? The Shoguns remained in control, their mouthpiece General Togo. Did they not realize that Russia, after Yalta, was mobilizing to invade too, and that a Berlin-like confrontation would result?

We were on the Maui beaches ready to go. Transports (APAs) lay just off the beaches to allow us, fully loaded, to practice climbing up and down on the rope ladders. Was there any discussion of our future? No, our task was just to get where we were going. On our training, and on fate itself, we would depend for survival.

Then the Miracle—we can go home!

Standing next to the communications Jeep, I heard something to the tune that a single, new super bomb had just been dropped on Hiroshima. The city was gone. All of my Japanese history lessons and the experience of watching the Bushido culture close at hand as a boy condensed into a, "Gus, the war is over." Col. Banks, our commander, exclaimed, "Come on Doc, you're full of it!" Guess not. The war was over! The Emperor, being realistic and knowing he was human after all, saw the inevitable and regained his omnipotence. We could all go home and not find ourselves in untenable positions as we fought to live another day.

I looked back later, and long after the My Lai massacre in Vietnam, recognized that our lots would have been similar. Could we as a Christian nation have dealt successfully with our guilt? I can't imagine the consequences. Young Americans, please listen. Harry Truman's lonely decision will, hopefully, rank as one of the greatest in history, as a *deciding*, not a *turning* point in time. Thanks, Harry. Guess these words would never have been written, had your wisdom not prevailed.

CHAPTER

9.

Boston Adventure

Next open door closed for good by Carol

It was time to go home and pick up life's threads. Overnight, our 24th Battalion decamped, and in a matter of days, after making sure that our parents knew we really were home, all were assigned close by in peaceful pursuits. I was sent to the Navy medical unit at Alameda Air Station. For six months, with Blue Beauty in motion, I luxuriated in my America—tennis, golf, and skiing—but pieces of my career had to be picked up. My fellow physicians at my stage of training were one step ahead of me, for they had already secured the precious residencies. Had they seen the war coming to such an abrupt end? I doubt it. I think they were more realistic, anticipating their discharge from the services, while I still lived one day at a time. And I still do, as I go with the winds.

In my case, the wind was Carol. Standing by the rope tow at the Sierra Club in Norden (near Donner Summit), I spotted this skier gliding towards me. I turned to Instructor Bill Klein, and said, "Who is that beautiful skier?" I was referring to more than skiing motions. "May I meet her?" That did it, and my future as a husband was in the works. At the same time, my future as a provider was in limbo and could no longer be put off. We were married six months later in Grace Cathedral in San Francisco, and the next episode in this real-life drama took off.

Had anything happened to change my pattern of taking one day at a time? Yes. For the first time, there were two of us. "One day at a time" would now always require a more detailed look at the long haul at stake. I still had to examine a next step, and it had to still follow my rule of keeping all the doors open until Carol and I would settle into a chosen life's work, together.

We open Boston's portal on our honeymoon

My intention to be exposed to other medical disciplines had not changed. The Boston City Hospital internship had been exciting, but it was time to go on. I had saved up enough money to allow a few months of exploration in Boston, it now obvious that I would be a surgeon. Years of surgical residency was the next step. I must still keep doors open for a specialty. My fascination with the mysteries of the sympathetic nervous system had increased. This had started in medical school when Dr. Livingston, a neurosurgeon at the University of Oregon, proved that a single small injection of anaesthetic into what he called the "trigger point" in a painful amputation stump could end the otherwise permanently debilitating phantom limb pain. Beyond this, the sympathectomy surgery of Reginald Smithwick in Boston could be dramatic in ending life-threatening hypertension. That was enough of a carrot for me. I could meet surgical residency demands, while entering a specialty that needed to be recognized and then available throughout the country. It seemed like the ground floor of something that an engineer, with his familiarity with wires and tracts might help develop, but how was I to break into the patriarchal system that was Boston?

Carol and I mixed serious business with fun as I camped, figuratively, on the doorstep of Boston Memorial Hospital (Boston University); I would not be dislodged. In the meantime, we drove around historic New England and upper New York State in our sporty, red Packard convertible, acquired for $600 during my internship. That price was the result of wartime gas limitations; the car had been rusting on blocks.

We often camped out in our pup tent in the unlikeliest of spots. One dark night, we were getting desperate for somewhere to stay in upper New York State. I saw a place, turned in to a driveway, then pitched the tent in the dark. We had a wonderful night's sleep until voices awakened us and Carol poked her head out. Low and behold, church-goers were waving at us, for we were squarely in their cemetery. In Bar Harbor, Maine, it was in the city dump, and in New Hampshire it was a football field, where we were told unceremoniously to "git."

Dr. Smithwick could not get me out of his hair. He was used to Harvard interns and residents in the hallowed Massachusetts General Hospital he had just left to be Massachusetts Memorial's Chief of Surgery. Interns there kept their gowns spotless. As third and second assistants, they had trouble at times seeing what the surgeon was doing. We Boston City Hospital residents, in tattered but clean surgical gowns, had been on the active surgical battlefront from day one as we assisted accomplished surgeons.

On top of this, I was a westerner, perhaps even a cowboy, from some small college on the West Coast! Didn't I know that a Bostonian thought that Worcester, 59 miles away, was the real West? What Dr. Reginald Smithwick would learn was that we true westerners are tenacious when we see a goal we must reach.

Dr. Smithwick's door finally opens; I walk in

In December, Dr. Smithwick caved in, but first I had to spend six months as a surgical researcher. So what? I would do anything to get in the operating room with him, and that is when a mechanism fell into place that would put me in the production line toward surgery of the sympathetic nervous system.

I was assigned as an assistant to Dr. Edward Free, who would eventually be Mr. Hypertension in the NIH in Washington. I worked with Harvard graduate Joe Stanton, and we quickly melded into a team. This was duck soup for me, because I was back into measuring, and then graphing, data, in this case having to do with surgical blood loss. We perfected the use of a special new dye, T1824 (Evans Blue), and were able to do wonders with it as we uncovered how the liver, as it builds plasma, really works. I became a seasoned researcher, manipulating the spectroscope with the best. I was also assigned a small room to test skin temperatures with a massive instrument that had been used for controls on airplane engines. This engineer was in heaven.

Carol won't be left behind

What did Carol do with her time? At a party, having been stuck in one corner with the ladies, and seeing the men in another corner having such a good time, she decided not to remain deprived. She took Pre-med courses at Boston University and kibitzed at Harvard third-year medical student classes in the hospitals. Disaster would lurk as she picked up a little information, especially when it touched her. At the Peter Bent Brigham Hospital, during rounds, iconic George Thorn was showing a child with nephrosis, her tissues edematous (swollen) as the result of streptococcal infection endemic on the East Coast but rare out West.

Carol remembered her own sick bout at age five when a fever of 105 was ominous and the doctors disagreed as to treatment—no sulfas or antibiotics existed then. Her meek pediatrician wanted to wait it out and hope for the best. Surgeon Krakow predicted that not to operate to remove infected tonsils and adenoids would likely be fatal. The courageous surgeon won. Carol's temperature dropped immediately to normal, and she fully recovered.

There is more to the story: The Brigham child also seemed to have survived her infection. Later on, though, the signs of kidney damage appeared and were now manifested as slowly fatal glomerular nephritis. This was the malady with which I had become so familiar in Dr. Addis's lab as a student at Stanford. Carol put two and two together. She was scared. So was I. To reassure her, on a Sunday morning I heated some vinegar (acetic acid) and added her urine. The heavy cloud that resulted left no doubt that the protein (albumin) component was high. We promptly went to the hospital lab, and again the test was positive, but there was something reassuring. With my centrifuge, I "spun down" particles that might be diagnostic in her urine. If there were casts or cells present consistent with kidney disease, my Addis training assured that I would recognize them. The specimen was beautifully clear. Dr. Addis had taught me that a heavy proteinuria like this is not seen with kidney disease, but with a benign syndrome, orthostatic proteinuria, where the protein appears only with patient activity in the upright (orthostatic) position. I was sure of the diagnosis, so when it was recommended that Dr. Williams, a Boston expert, be consulted I said, "Not on your life." I had seen enough of these so-called experts to be fully disenchanted. I was sure Dr. Williams didn't know one cast from another in the urinary sediment, and to him Tom Addis was likely to be considered just another western aberration. Only when we went West to my urological residency did I ask Bud Persike, like me trained by the wonderful man, to see Carol. I offered no opinion. He called me promptly to confirm the good news. Once again, "Thank you, Thomas Addis."

A second episode at Peter Bent Brigham has a longer history. Carol was listening to the famous Dr. Kolff, inventor of the artificial kidney. He announced that there were three questions he wished to be asked. These would be rewarded with his signed original monograph. Two of the questioners received their prizes. The third question lay in limbo. Carol, having been told each day of my work relating to pulmonary embolism, nudged the student next to her and said to him, "Why  don't you ask how the blood is kept from clotting in the machine?"

"You ask it," he said. Carol laughed as she responded, "Are you kidding? They'll throw me out." This student won the monograph. He should have handed it to Carol. Thirty years later in Dr. Frank Hinman's home in San Francisco, I told guest Dr. Kolff about the incident. A signed monograph arrived at our home two days later. It has a place of honor on my office wall.

Dr. Smithwick keeps his promise; I am in surgical whites again

Dr. Smithwick dragged his feet getting me into a house officer's whites. More than once I reminded him of his promise. I finally was made the lone resident in the Framingham Boston University Hospital at the margin of the city. I was on my surgical way. Three months later I became chief resident in the big hospital, charged with full patient care: IV's, surgical schedule, and assistant to Drs. Smithwick, Whitelaw, and Graham, who perhaps expected me to follow in their footsteps.

An unnoticed door opens

Two seminal events took place during my eighteen months at Massachusetts Memorial Hospital with its Boston University Medical School faculty. The first would open up for me a lifetime of stimulating events, as I found myself pioneering an entirely new science that would affect all fields of medicine and surgery. It was about time, for morbidity, and even mortality, was out of control everywhere from a lack of understanding of the chemical components in lost body secretions, and the need for their prompt replacement with suitable solutions. Salt and water alone were far from enough, and I would find myself on the road for years bringing this message. The new science would be called Fluid Electrolyte Balance. It started this way.

I inadvertently become a pioneer in fluid electrolyte balance

I was strolling through the surgical ward, looking a subject for a blood test in our research study of blood regeneration. My eye caught an inert patient just an arm's length away, festooned with IV tubing and drainage catheters. Dr. Douglas Farmer had just come from the Massachusetts General Hospital to be an assistant professor of surgery. This was his ward.

"Dr. Farmer, what is the diagnosis?"

"He is dying in hepatic (liver) coma. He is icteric (jaundiced) and his plasma proteins are half of normal as a result, and thus the edema (swollen tissues). To make things worse, he is the father of a medical student."

"May I take a crack at him, Dr. Farmer?"

"Of course. He's yours; we've given up."

It was obvious to me that he was overloaded with fluid. This was a day when the term "fluid balance" was almost unknown. The diagnosis of edema depended entirely on the eye of the physician. I was just beginning to tap into a massive defect in care, where normal saline (9 grams of salt/liter) in an IV was deemed the accepted universal antidote for all hydration problems, the physician focusing only on the urine output as the critical measurement.

I stopped all IVs. It took just three days for Mr. Feldman to wake up. His edema disappeared as his legs approached normal, but the most sticking change was a serum protein that went from 3 to a normal 6 mg./liter, while he had eaten nothing. Protein was clearly not being created. It was being diluted! On the tenth day, with body water and tissues back to normal, he was discharged to home.

So, what had happened? I don't recall why he was in the hospital, but it was clear that he had been massively overloaded with salt and water. The swollen liver's ducts were blocked, and cell mechanisms were compromised. Protein formation by the liver cells had stopped. The hemoglobin, freed as normal red cell replacement occurred, was trapped. Jaundice was the result. It was a case of *overload*, a condition I would contend with repeatedly in the years ahead.

Did the concept of a scale to weigh the excess water in this inert patient enter my thoughts then? No. I had not the least idea of the massive part of my medical life ahead that this element would play. Experts in that day, such as Francis Moore at Massachusetts General, and Carl Moyer in the Midwest, had not yet emphasized the true problem, but they must have known about it. Only in Minnesota in 1943 had the now renowned professor of surgery, Owen Wangensteen, seen the truth, as he constructed a massive scale, much like that in a butcher shop of that day. No one took notice. This lack of acceptance occurred again in 1948, when his article appeared in the New England Journal. This man is a legend today, for he introduced the first effective tube that with suction decompresses the obstructed bowel. It is still a staple known as Wangensteen Suction. His equally great contribution to body weight and water is still unrecognized.

Something, however, was happening to me that would intensify through the years. Recognizing a problem and then solving it was not new to me. It was by then a habit. What was new is the matter of being *effective*. This became my mantra and has remained so to the present day. It is, in the end, all that counts! I'm sure Mr. Feldman would have agreed.

Fatal pulmonary embolization is tackled and prevented

This second sequence is also the story of another "awakening." With my research time completed, I was at this point the surgical resident, and I had acquired a chore that was just plain burdensome. Recall that I had flunked the exam for a Thorndyke internship because I knew nothing about the syndrome of thrombophlebitis and pulmonary embolism and its often fatal outcome. Here I was with 12 of my 120 patients in that state. This required that I administer the anticoagulant Heparin intravenously every eight hours. That would have been easy, but I had to do a complicated bleeding and clotting test before each injection, and I was back in the lab again. This turned out to be a break point in my life.

Now that my medical training and experience had reached a certain level of proficiency, I would find my engineering principles at times filling in gaps in the medical knowledge I gained in school and on the job, allowing me to see things in a different light from my colleagues. I would recognize problems unnoticed by others and then, as the tinkerer by habit, try to solve them.

All medical students are familiar with the tendency for blood to rapidly clot when allowed to stand, thereby spoiling a specimen. By keeping the blood in motion, it tends to stay fluid, but was anyone considering that motion is a good idea? How about just speeding the flow through the big main vein in the lower leg, the calf, the section prone to inflammation, particularly with inactivity during surgery and after. Why hadn't this been thought of by others familiar with the clotting mechanisms?

Our hematology department was known worldwide, so I trod lightly, but I had one great advantage. Dr. Fries, my research boss, had trained me well in research processes, so that when I broached my idea to Dr. Smithwick, he said, "Why not. Go ahead. You and Dr. Fries know the ropes."

The idea? Daniel Bernoulli, father of fluid dynamics, had made it very clear that the velocity of a fluid in a pipe could be markedly increased with very little change in the pipe's diameter. A vein is not a rigid pipe, but could we apply this principle, and speed the flow in the single large deep vein, the site of clot formation? We had the tools, the Evans Blue dye that I injected many times each day, and the radio-opaque dye used for kidney X-rays. We could track as well as see the flow when pressure was applied. Dr. Fries found us aviators' pressure puttees (tight  restraints) used in high-speed airplane dives. With our first try, the speed of venous blood flow doubled, and this was proved over and over again. The incidence of pulmonary embolism was cut in half as Ace bandages, and then snug stockings, created by Bauer and Black, changed surgical care forever. Today, airline travelers on long flights, wearing these stockings, no longer have to tramp the aisles, as long as heel and toe exercises, while seated, speed the venous flow and protect them from blood clotting and embolization.

Everyone and his brother at the hospital were named as authors as the findings were reported, a medical game with which I would become increasingly familiar, the paper appearing in the New England Journal of Medicine. I was by then in San Francisco, having gone west to my urological residency. My name did not even make a footnote, yet

I was surprised that I didn't really care. Why? Because it was becoming obvious that my parents' lessons had stuck.

The lasting satisfaction comes in just knowing you are *effective*. Approval by others was not in my personal equation as I followed my intent, corny as it sounds, to do something for someone each day. As a doctor, how easy this was proving to be. I had made the right choice that day nine years earlier in the Zete House. This first step in Problem Recognition, Solution, and finally being Effective had put me already ahead in the ball game of life, and it provided me with added stimulus to keep following my instincts and to act on them promptly.

As I think about it and recognize that in my case this partnership of engineering and medicine has seemed so productive, why haven't the medical schools sought out engineers wishing to be doctors, to fill the roles of bioengineers who can be counted on to ask the "dumb questions?"

I choose a new specialty—Urology

As my first year of residency was ending, Dr. Smithwick suggested that I consider another surgical specialty, for in this very hospital the search for a medical cure for hypertension was paying off. That was obvious to me, for in my lab I was testing an American plant extract, *Veratrum Veridi*, its blood pressure effects being so potent as to be dangerous if not controlled. Other less violent medications were bound to follow.

Was I disappointed? Yes, for I had had wide experience with the effectiveness of our surgery, many times performed on important Americans. I treasure a first edition of the physician stamps that Postmaster General Hannigan presented to me as he went home, unoperated because of kidney damage associated with hypertension. I remember it as a sad day.

The triumphs of surgical sympathectomy, although winning the battle, were losing the war. I recall doing a routine physical exam on a twenty-four year old patient being seen in follow-up. I had become proficient in examining retinas, the windows to measure vascular damage going on all over the body. His retinas, the windows into vascular damage from high blood pressure, were normal. I wondered why I was seeing him as a patient. I then looked into his record. One year earlier his eye grounds were hemorrhagic "Grade 4s" and a death notice, for his systolic blood pressure was then "malignant," in the 300 range. The Smithwick Splanchnicectomy had won the day. I was convinced of its value, but it was too late. Medical control seemed assured, surgery no longer needed.

As doors still were open to any surgical specialty, orthopedics and chest tempted me, as their chiefs welcomed this energetic westerner. It was the urologist, Sam Vose, likable as well as famous, who put me on the track I had not before taken seriously, despite the hopes of my Uncle Bert Meads.

It then occurred to me that Tom Addis would have his way after all, for I had become so familiar with kidneys as I retracted them out of the way in our sympathetic nervous system surgeries. Why not go one step further and repair them as a life work?

The doors would still be open as to where and how I would practice

Uncle Bert Meads wished me to be a student and he the "preceptor," a practice then accepted by the Urological Boards, but this was no match for the University of California across the Bay, where Dr. Frank Hinman, perhaps the leading urologist in the world, had his residency program. I applied in the face of talented competition. Frank Hinman Jr., I believe, had a say in the decision, for what little contact we had had suggested that he too had the roving mind of an innovator. I was accepted, and the wheel turned again. Opportunity existed nearby in Boston, but it was time to return to the West, and time for Carol and me to begin our family where future grandparents could be shareholders. The decision was uncontested, save by Bostonians who, when told of our leaving, said only, "Why?" After all, to them, the West was still wild, confirmed a little by the free spirits they had come to know, Carol and Dick.

We didn't think our beloved Packard convertible, the Red Bomber, could make it home safely, for it had been without cover and so was traumatized on the icy streets and in the snow. We left it in Boston, its home at the start. A racy, green Pontiac convertible carried us west. We again camped along the way, making the most of our freedom before settling down to family life ahead. Our new home would be upstairs in a new duplex just a few blocks from the Medical Center in San Francisco.

CHAPTER

10.

Urology in San Francisco

California urological residency

My residency began in Franklin Hospital, just over the hill from our apartment. I found myself in another world. Open surgery was still the order of the day, but I was also introduced to the trans-urethral resection of the prostate and the fluid risks it entailed. One of the first instrumental procedures in all of surgery, it required a clear fluid to expose and remove prostatic tissue in pieces rather than as a whole through an incision. This fluid, at even the moderate flow pressure required, could seep into the circulation as bleeding was stanched by electrocoagulation. The fluid could not contain salt, for a short-circuit would occur. Thus, only water could be the irrigant. Therein lay the dilemma. If a fine resection was done as obstructive tissue was removed, the danger of fluid absorption increased. The fluid would be picked up by red cells, making them swell and rupture, their hemoglobin freed and filtered through the kidneys. The hemoglobin would then be concentrated in the excretory tubules, blocking them, with a resulting kidney failure that would require ten days to repair itself and be able to create urine flow. This time frame was critical to patient survival. The lesion was described as acute tubular necrosis (ATN), or lower nephron nephrosis, likely to be fatal for reasons not then understood.

As I look back, I still find it hard to believe that I was immediately faced with this problem when a resident's TURP (Trans-Urethral Resection of the Prostate) case did shut down. The accepted treatment was to give normal saline (salt at 9 grams per liter) to replace insensible perspiration (800 cc's) and anticipate a daily urine output of 1,000 cc's or more. The idea was to *push* the kidneys to make urine. This misunderstanding of kidney function could be fatal.

Thomas Addis's teaching now came into play. Kidney repair could not be rushed, for it would remain shut down, the patient becoming "anuric" (no urine) or "oliguric" (just a few cc's each day). I searched the medical literature. I was not surprised to find that pulmonary edema (flooded lungs) was the usual cause of death, this being the final stage of heart failure. I had no doubt we were dealing with acute fluid overload, not chronic as with my Feldman Boston case, and heart failure could be the result.

We save a life

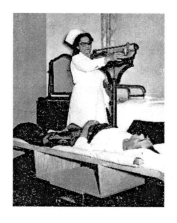

I was now in full charge; the patient was my responsibility. Within hours of surgery, the IV's were stopped. My problem: I must know his immediate weight, but he could not stand on the scale. My solution: I went to the garage of my Stanyon Street home, revved up my new Shopsmith, a machine that could do everything, and turned out a plywood litter that would fit the large Fairbanks "potato scale" found in every supply room. Effective? You bet it was, and through the years to immediately follow, in the East Bay, I carried the litter in the back of my car, ready to be used in hospital consultations where a Fairbanks scale was always at hand.

I had to promptly decide on a survival plan. I knew that a base need for calories with a patient in bed without any physical exertion is 800 calories per day. Also, I recognized that a gram of protein, as it is metabolized, produces four calories and also creates a half gram of water. A gram of fat would yield 9 calories and a little more than a gram of water. Thus, in round figures, the daily need of 800 calories would be met as 800 cc's of new water was produced. This balanced the insensible perspiration loss of 800 cc's, occurring from the lungs with breathing, but there was a catch: the tissue-to-water ratio was changing as tissue was catabolized, changing into energy and waste products, leaving new water that might act as slight overload. This was something I could not chance. Therefore, he was allowed to lose one pound of body weight per day (about 500 cc's). I would keep him on the dry side. Fluid intake would not be allowed, orally or by vein, until diuresis (full urine flow) at ten days. No patient complaint of thirst could influence me.

From that day on, every lower nephron nephrosis patient survived, in other hospitals as well, as they asked for help. The circle of cause-to-cure was completed when we wrote the report. My assistant resident, John Huffer, presented the report at the urological meeting in Sun Valley, while I had to stay home and stand guard.

My third intent, to be effective, was fulfilled as word spread throughout the country. ATN, although to be avoided at all costs, was now tamed, and the TURP was more widely used, as it became the standard prostatic operation.

Later, when I questioned residents as to the importance of body weight control within surgery, I found it accepted as doctrine. No one knew its source. My joy in just being effective was reward enough.

Fluid electrolyte balance again takes hold

The three years of residency was a continuum of my education in clinical body physiology. In private practice, hundreds of times I was called to see patients, often comatose, and was able to make them well again. This was a whole new world, and it would continue to expand until Dr. Kolff created the first dialysis unit, which was later made smaller and practical by fellow Stanfordite Belding Scribner at Washington University in Seattle. This had plusses that far outnumbered the minuses. My consultive fluid balance practice ended in the mid-1960s. By dialyzing a patient, whatever the fluid-electrolyte imbalance, the machine would correct everything. It still does this today.

This chapter is really a history of an immense advance in patient care. I will try to illustrate it by events in my learning curve that must have paralleled that of other physicians who also found themselves trying to master this new discipline. It was the creation of the flame photometer that made all things possible. It appeared in medical centers about 1947. In another five years it was available everywhere, but it was still something of a curiosity when I came to San Francisco. Therefore, I relied primarily on my own bedside tests, with my bottle of reagents designed by Belding Scribner always at hand. This made it possible for me to make an instant chloride measurement, so valuable in determining the make-up of secretions lost in tubes, bowel leaks as fistulas, and

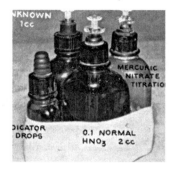

diarrheas. The chlorides in the urine were often critical to a diagnosis and therapy. I could begin treatment almost instantly, not having to rely on the laboratory. In San Francisco, as well as later in the East Bay, photometer readings were slow to be obtained, so I relied on the handy bedside set most of the time and used the photometer readings as confirmation.

Too bad the urine sample was discarded

There was a humorous mistake, which did no harm, but which might have been revealing if it hadn't happened at all. I had been sent a Kaiser patient with the most serious of congenital lesions—bilateral border-line kidney failure as a probable result of a posterior urethral valve at birth (I will describe this later). A violent diarrhea had resulted from an antibiotic meant to treat his urinary tract infection, to the point that he was severely dehydrated, as infusions could not keep up with the fluid losses. His kidneys were no more than thin shells, and he was only in his late forties! I will never know how he had survived so long. He wouldn't have, in his boiler room job, had his wife not sent him to work with many Thermoses of vegetable and fruit juices each day to slake his thirst. Tom Addis, with his low-protein vegetarian diet, would have approved.

My job was to rehydrate him, and bring the diarrhea under control. How much potassium did he need and how much was too much? The flame photometer was still in its infancy and we had much to learn about this ion.

Now to my point. Always the investigator, I tried never to miss the opportunity to learn as I worked on these critical cases. The patient recovered and was to go home. As he walked out of the hospital door, he had a fatal heart attack. I wasn't so sure that the diagnosis was correct, for this could have been a cardiac arrest from a serum potassium either too low or too high. I had the means to find out, I thought.

From day one, I had taken a blood sample, spun it to separate out the red cells, and then preserved the plasma. It was as yellow as urine. My intent was to have the overworked photometer measure the potassium levels as I reflected back on the patient's course. To be sure that the specimens were not forgotten or misplaced, I put them in a rack by the lab window. My mistake! I should have written somewhere, "Don't touch." Our veteran nurse and trusted mistress of the lab for at least thirty years decided on this very day that the samples were just old urines and should be thrown out. They were, and my rushing to get them was too late. Could a major discovery about the use of potassium have resulted? I will never know, but the correct use of potassium had by then become a passion for me.

The principles of potassium replacement and body weight put to the test by daughter Kathy

We knew very little about the potassium content of a diarrhea. The first real study of electrolytes in all secretions had just been published by James Gamble. This was a monumental step forward. I rejoiced in it as a winner. A surprise was the high content in the infant garden-variety diarrhea. I put this data to the test in my own home.

Kathleen, just seven months old, was suddenly taken with an intense, watery diarrhea. The possibility of serious dehydration was real. Dr. Jacobs, pediatric professor and friend, took one look and said, "Into the hospital."

"No way," was my retort, "because I will be called in to consult, and I can do this right here at home. I'll make you a deal. You and I know the danger is not the bug, which you can treat, but the dehydration. If I don't let that happen, may Kathleen stay home?" He knew of my work with body water and weight, and immediately gave in.

First, I took a sample of the diarrhea to the lab and measured its electrolytes. The surprise was that each liter contained a gram of potassium. This is three to four times the amount found in other bowel secretions. Now, to the library, for I must replace this loss cc. for cc. Again a surprise. Plain skim milk was it, but milk was thought to make the diarrhea worse. So what! I would balance weight and water, for this was my charge.

Here was our homegrown pattern. Believing that vomiting was likely to occur if we pushed things, I calculated that a teaspoon, no more, every hour night and day would do it. The monitor was her body weight. As long as it stayed within a pound of normal, we were winners. Dr. Jacobs was satisfied. Carol and I played musical chairs, with her on the job during the day, and us sharing the job at night. Weighing was accomplished with our small bedside scale, parents weighing themselves each time, then weighing again holding Kathleen, something any parent can do. Three days did it. Dr. Jacobs volunteered he had never before seen such a rapid recovery.

The tinkerer's mind latched on to an obvious corollary: Why don't pediatricians teach each parent to use weight as a guide when a diarrhea appears, the skim milk regime applied, and the need for hospitalization determined by weight loss? I doubt it has made the manual even today.

The Leslie affair—another potassium victory

My next potassium challenge patient, a valued PG & E employee, appeared comatose and severely dehydrated after a femoral fracture ten days earlier. It is an axiom that trauma of this magnitude is poorly handled by the male. Bowel peristalsis (contractions) shuts down (ileus), and gastric tube drainage is a necessity until bowel sounds return. His drainage seemed not to have worked, but regardless of my not having a reliable history, Ralph required immediate and dramatic treatment. Intravenous salt and water was the first step, its rate and volume controlled by weight change, as the Fairbanks Scale and my litter became his bedside companion.

With things for the moment going well, I took Mrs. Leslie aside to ask her what she thought had gone wrong, when therapy seemed to be up to code. "Was the tube working well?"

"Yes, in fact he enjoyed his Cokes," was her answer.

"What did you say?

"He drank gallons of everything from juices to Cokes to water."

The cause was now clear. He had in effect self-dialyzed himself. These solutions would take body water, salt, and potassium with them as they returned through the tube to the drainage bottle. Owen Wangensteen must have been spinning in his grave at such a misuse of his sacred suction tube, but our therapy was now unquestioned. Salt and water coverage we could accomplish over the three days I had allowed for recovery, but potassium was the enigma, for it had been lost as well in the stomach juice, and its aggressive use was still feared by clinicians. What I had most to fear was not a low reading from the lab, but a fatally low T-wave on the EKG (heart tracing).

At 24 hours, the T-wave started to flatten and disappear. Ralph suddenly woke up, too, a coincidence I believed. Potassium was added in high concentrations to the IV infusions immediately. Yet, it required another two days for the T-wave to reach its normal contour. Twice as much potassium as salt was infused to return cellular metabolism to normal.

From that day on, potassium would be my greatest concern. There had to be a better way to give it, for my supplements made up by the pharmacy were crude.

As a resident, I wasn't allowed to accept remuneration, but PG&E insisted that there be some reward for returning their special employee to his job. How about a 10-cubic foot refrigerator? After all Carol was an accomplice as she supported my three days at Ralph's bedside. It was delivered the afternoon that Ralph was delivered home.

"Wunderkind" Krupp takes the stage

It seems strange and perhaps even wonderful that the potassium story for all America and the world continued to be centered right here in the Far West, far from Boston gurus. Marcus Krupp, Stanford internist and a mentor for me, did something spectacular for potassium as a saver of lives, particularly in areas where the fear of potassium remained. I always believed that our work was complementary, he developing methods in the University lab, I then putting them to "on the job" use, supplemented by my scale and litter and bedside tests. We both traveled widely in the State to spread the word about this wondrous new science affecting every stage of patient care.

What did Marcus do? He designed an ampule-encased solution combining potassium with calcium and magnesium, all essential ions lost in secretions. He called it the KMC ampule. It changed the name of the game everywhere. Fear of its correct, controlled use dissipated rapidly. The KMC ampule eventually disappeared as solutions appeared primed with potassium, now

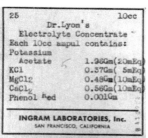

Marcus Krupp's KMC Ampule

designated "replacement solutions," as they are today. What made it foolproof was the balancing of calcium and potassium. If the ampule's contents were, by mistake, injected into a vein without being diluted in a liter of solution, the dangerous potassium would be neutralized by the calcium. This was a remarkable example of a "do it now" innovator being marvelously effective.

Body weight measurements go on hold

There was still something missing. Easy and accurate body weight measurement was not discussed. It would have to wait until it would become practical. Was I planning all this? Absolutely not. I had enough on my learning platter to more than fill my days, often with "little" things, so the big things had to wait.

Residency and mentors

Residency is a wonderful time. Your ever-present and watchful mentors have just one intent—to draw the very best out of you. There is no time for slackers. One or two mistakes could be tolerated in the learning process. A third was "fatal." These residents were fired with the hope that this punishment would be great enough for them to learn their lesson. I now doubt they did.

My first contact with kidney surgery was a surprise. The patient would be turned on the side and strapped in place. The anesthesiologist would then struggle to be sure the compressed lower lung was filled with air. The incision was wide, far wider than I believed necessary, conditioned as I was in Boston. Too many vessels and nerves were encountered, the nerves stripped, and thus later could be sources of severe pain for days, sometimes for years. Postoperative pain required heavy sedation and limited body motion, both detrimental to recovery. Complaining was not my choice, however; somewhere inside the wheels were turning. I would do something about this when the time was ripe.

Our other surgical procedures seemed to me quite beautiful. Donald Smith was pioneering the repair of the congenital penis deformity, hypospadias, that bound down the organ so it often looked like a female clitoris. Our instruments, the endoscopes, were beautiful as we examined bladders and catheterized ureters to study kidney function. The IVP (intravenous pyelogram), created in Germany, was the glorious standard to see kidneys and ureters clearly. And finally, the Hinman preoccupation with the kidney as the primary focus suited me well, for Tom Addis was always at my shoulder. The PSP (phenolsulfonphthalein) test, which provided information presently obtained with expensive isotope scans, was the backbone. The PSP test has never been surpassed.

The PSP test awakening; "Do it"

One day when I was working at the "pee bench," Dr. John Schulte, partner with Dr. Hinman and a chip off the old block, passed by. He was just "John," as I was "Dick." I remarked, "John, why do we have to do this PSP test on everyone? In Boston it was considered inconsistent." Without breaking stride, John said, "Do it." By "doing it now" thousands of times, I soon became a believer and its defender.

What in the end shot it down? The test required four specimens at 30-minute intervals. The lab technicians often mixed these up, and the doctor, frustrated by uneven results, ceased to use it. But because a Hinman man always did his own testing, his results were reliable. I learned to require just a single specimen, and found the test consistent and accurate. How I would miss it, were I practicing today!

Frank Hinman, mentor—the man and his "eight steps"

It was evident from the first that I was now part of a unique system, designed by a man easily the world's authority on many urological problems, especially the kidney that is damaged by obstruction (hydronephrosis). He first worked in the lab with animals, and then in the operating room, testing and proving his theories. If one could be classified a genius, he was that. This brings me to my point: He was also known for his "eight steps," a list of things always to be considered before any diagnosis is entertained, and these steps were so simple! In other words, marshal your facts, no matter how obvious they might seem, before even considering a diagnosis.

This is within the capabilities of anyone no matter his intellectual capacities; they are not complicated:

1. General history and physical examination
2. Urological history
3. Abdominal palpation findings
4. Genitalia examination
5. Rectal examination
6. Three-glass urine test
7. PSP kidney function test
8. KUB (X-ray of kidneys, ureters, and bladder)

According to Google, this test is now known as the "Valentine Test." Correction please! It is the "Hinman Eight Steps."

There were other rules of conduct. The Hinman system left no room for guesswork. At one monthly presentation, Dr. Hinman as always there, the chief resident presented his case, where a retrograde pyelogram (visualization of a kidney with dye expressed through a catheter) had demonstrated a filling defect in the pelvis of a kidney. It could be a small tumor requiring removal, or just a bubble of air. There was silence as we all waited for the results of a repeat study to be absolutely sure the tumor was really there before operating. That was a cardinal Hinman rule—there would be no guessing. The resident proudly stated that his surgery had removed a true tumor. Dr. Hinman's comment, "Next case," eliminated any discussion, and left no doubt that the resident had flunked the guesswork test, and after three years of training!

The checklist was a natural for me. On my ward, every patient had a check sheet with his record hanging on his bed. It was, therefore, so easy not to make a mistake, as my senior resident found when he tried to trap me time and again. He finally gave up, and our friendship deepened through the years, for he knew I could be trusted.

The Hypogravic Urine—an inadvertent discovery

An 11-year old boy with the appearance of an old man was admitted comatose to my ward in the County Hospital. He was obviously severely dehydrated. His kidney tests were those of advanced kidney failure. It took 48 hours to awaken him and gain a history. This episode had been repeated many times, almost since birth. I would later appreciate that Kelly was in reality my first contact with the results of a congenital posterior urethral valve (PUV), the most serious of all congenital lesions. Further, it was still almost unknown to urologists, although Hugh Young, father of urology at Johns Hopkins, had described it many years earlier.

109

Something else was wrong, however. Every text stated unequivocally that the specific gravity, or density, of urine is always fixed at 1.010 as any type of kidney failure progresses. Kelly's urine density was not the classic 1.010. It was lower, at 1.004, even though the demands of dehydration were still severe. A normal kidney would attain a urine density as high as 1.036 with this degree of dehydration. What was I missing? Every reading was still 1.004 with my densitometer. To compound my surprise, on a second entry a few weeks later, Kelly's urine density was even lower, at 1.002, almost water (1.000). Kelly died peacefully.

Now I had a bear by the tail, for tradition was being assaulted. I had best wait for more evidence, but it took another several years to acquire my third case. I published the data with the title of *The Hypogravic Urine*, breaking the rule that all kidney failures could produce only a urine with a specific gravity of 1.010. Was it ever noticed? Rarely! Only one accomplished physiologist noticed the article, and his complimentary report appeared as an editorial in the prime investigative journal, *The Journal of Medicine*.

Even today, few urologists and only an occasional nephrologist knows that a density lower than 1.010 in a dehydrated patient signifies obstruction, and thus is amenable to urological repair, perhaps life-saving, while the 1.010 retains its dire prognosis. Habit, even in science, is difficult to change.

Is it humor or bad luck? I chose humor for Dad and Polaroid

My father believed that one should not invest in stocks without having a special expertise in that particular field. The Crash of 1929 served only to make him more gun-shy and not heed his own rules. The rule was, "Don't invest unless you are familiar with the science involved and the product produced."

I had heard about a radically new camera and went to the store to examine it. This Polaroid camera was clearly the engineer working with the photographer. I was both. Eastman would not be able to catch up with Polaroid for a long time, I believed.

I called Dad, defending my use of his rule, and suggested he put in $5,000. No dice! I didn't have $5,000 to risk, and was concentrating on just the day ahead anyway. Did I miss my calling?

CHAPTER

11.

I Practice with Dr. Meads

My year with mentor Uncle Bert

My residency completed, without hesitation I made the choice to pass up opportunity in academia for the privilege of caring for patients one on one. That was a choice I would never regret. I joined Uncle Bert Meads in Oakland, the man who had brought me into the world. How fortunate to have such a natural next step.

During my year with Uncle Bert, I trod lightly as I continued to learn, for he was truly a master of his trade. He put the final touches on my ability as a resectionist of the prostate as well as the open-surgical perineal prostatectomy, which even today with all of our non-invasive advances is a worthy competitor. However, I am most beholden to him for demanding that I trace every X-ray. In so doing, he was sure I had completed the work-up of each of his patients. I was responsible, as in my residency, for histories and physicals. Uncle Bert was now my mentor-preceptor. But the payoff for me was something else. These traced X-rays served to make me examine carefully each film, the tracing then ending up in the patient's record. Though not my original intention, these tracings allowed me later to carry on intensive patient studies without having to dig through hospital files each time. What a blessing this habit has been as hospital X-rays have either been destroyed or made difficult to recover, on microfilm stored far away.

I have repeatedly tried to interest residents in this practice. I've had no takers, as they wonder where I have sprung from. Besides, their laptops have it all on the record after all.

113

I move to Berkeley and begin solo practice

It was time to be on my own. Berkeley, with its medical community of professor-caliber escapees from the constrictions of academia, seemed to me to be the apex of medical care. It emanated out of Alta Bates Hospital and was equaled by Oakland's Children's Medical Center. I couldn't have been more content, although my practice would grow slowly. My three girls would have the advantage of Berkeley schools, then top-of-the line, as well as the experience of growing up in an integrated community far ahead of its time.

Practice growth, faithfully graphed in Dad's fashion, was a straight line, at a new patient per month, each month. Only 12 new patients at the year's end would discourage most starting doctors, but I found the trend consistent, and sure enough, at five years sixty new patients per month were seen. The mix had changed, for children were now appearing in numbers as a new subspecialty was in the making, Pediatric Urology. It was a natural offshoot––not something really new.

I teach everywhere

Consultations, not strictly urological, had pyramided as fluid-electrolyte balance was emerging as a science. Practitioners were rapidly accepting that they could and must do a better job. The new Academy of General Practice, guided by my neighbor Bill Rodgers, pushed this education. I had to travel. I was happiest, of course, at the wheel of my car. I taught as far away as Palm Desert. It was an exciting time, as new knowledge was welcomed. This was especially true as Pediatrics came forward. Hundreds of presentations on such as the pediatric emergency, testicular torsion, focused on work dear to my heart, made possible by Children's Hospital as it encouraged these advances. Those were wonderful days, and I could still be at home and at play with my family. Could anyone ask for anything more?

Along the way, iconic John Lattimer at New York's Columbia Presbyterian Hospital asked me to join him as the professor in the new specialty of Pediatric Urology. It had all the perks—money, importance, and travel abroad.

My prompt answer was, "John, I am flattered, but no thank you. I must not miss the most important years in my lifetime with Carol and with my girls as they become women." I still cherish that decision.

The tinkerer story goes on. It wasn't long before I was in over my head, taking patients out of what at times were life-threatening conditions, where ignorance as to the use of fluids and electrolytes was the culprit. Some were sent from far away to Oakland to local surgeons, who were still in need of guidance. I would get the call for help, often in the middle of the night. My litter was doing yeoman duty, but I was flagging. Something had to be done to lighten that load, and it had become clear that I was alone in this endeavor. At UC San Francisco, Jim Hopper, a forward-seeing pathologist, had, in 1948, acquired a scale from a packing company and tried to adapt it for the seriously ill. Its size destroyed any chance for success, because it was too large for hospital elevators. Such a little thing can destroy a great idea.

The InBed Scale is created

I must have at hand a practical scale that would be easy for nurses to handle, and be located on each hospital floor. I went to two national scale companies and was promptly turned down. Once again, this was nothing new to me. The solution was still entirely in my hands. The engineer took over, for machine shop work in college had been a joy. I located a small machine shop, Acme, on East 14th street in Oakland, and made the necessary drawings. The owner was impressed. Together we went ahead and built the scale by adapting the Fairbanks scale, creating a litter on top that would be non-obtrusive on a ward and easily moved about. The litter would be pulled down in such a way that it would rest on the bed. The scale's heavy platform slid under the bed for balance. The patient then could be drawn onto the litter as attendants manned the sheets. We called it the InBed Scale. It required only a finish paint job to be done.

I told the owner that he should get the patent. I saw it as not only of marketing value to the owner, but as a teaching tool for nurses to use and in turn educate the physicians as to the new science in the important relationship of body weight and water. It did just that. The patent was secured, I later learned. I was content to accept that I was effective, if the scale would make its way to where it was so badly needed. The fluid-electrolyte science now had wheels. It would get the lubrication of understanding. I was completing the open circle that Owen Wangensteen had created, but it had taken ten years to accomplish this. The appearance of the scale in Oakland hospitals assured me that it was really on the market. Obviously, sales were taking place. I learned that the InBed Scale was rapidly accepted throughout the country and abroad. It changed fluid electrolyte balance forever. I was effective.

The Anterior Retroperitoneal Incision is introduced

The second innovation needed was in the manner we approach the kidney for any surgery of it or the adrenal gland. As I started practice, I had no choice but to meet the demands of the Standard of Care and use the surgery accepted throughout the world. This was the flank incision with the limitations I have already described. I had to be patient, waiting for the unusual patient, who without any doubt would be best served by an operation allowing the supine (face up) position.

It took two years of patience. A Chinese American woman, all of 110 pounds, required removal of an infection-filled kidney and ureter of tuberculous origin. The flank position was out of the question, for a spill of tubercle bacilli from the upper lung to the lower was an unacceptable risk. The new approach thus could stand litigation, as malpractice lawyers were becoming numerous.

The Anterior Incision, really an extended Pearl incision with which I was so familiar, coupled with a second, small lower-right-quadrant incision, allowed me to complete the operation in one hour. On the surgical floor at dinnertime, my patient had a cigarette or two and a small dinner. Nurses were incredulous. They came in to see the incision to be sure this wasn't a joke. From that day on, kidney and ureter surgeries were pure joy for me.

With a dozen successful cases under my belt, I reported on the new procedure, naming it "The Retroperitoneal Incision." At presentation to the Urological Western Section, it won First Prize for Scientific Advancement. Was it immediately adopted by my profession? Not on your life. It would take much longer than I had anticipated. John Barry, Professor of Urology in Oregon, told me in 1995 that he had just discovered my paper written forty years earlier. The procedure was a joy for him. It made the removal of a kidney for transplant so untraumatic and rapid, it competed well with the longer laparoscopic procedures now in vogue. The almost pain-free postoperative course allowed for early mobilization and early return home.

The Problem was defined and a Solution provided, yet being effective was not that easy. Could I have done better by traveling as a Visiting Professor to spread the word? Perhaps, but my day-to-day responsibilities to patients at home denied me that luxury, a small price to pay for such an advance to be in place for years to come.

"Stress" brain tumor is a just a "happening," thankfully

All was not peaches and cream. The stress resulting from competing in a specialty well-entrenched throughout the East Bay was part of the bargain. I tried to neutralize it by family hours, physical exertions on the tennis court, and vacations in the Del Mar surf, but the stress of reality occasionally broke through.

On coming to Berkeley, one strong incentive was the belief that my training made me competitive. The two urologists in the other

Berkeley urology office were firmly ensconced, both having practiced there throughout the war years. How could I break in? I hoped that my years of training with Dr. Hinman would make the difference, while Donald Smith's teaching was already providing the impetus that was making pediatrics an ever-growing part of my practice. Believing I could add something new, I even went to the trouble of making photos with the just-invented Polaroid camera, putting the photos on my consultation notes until, one day, John Blum (my greatest supporter) said, "Dick forget it. Just give me the diagnosis and tell me what you want to do."

One morning, as I prepared for surgery at Merritt Hospital, I was hit with a visual blast of "central scotoma"—sort of a sharp flash of light. My first thought was that I had a brain tumor. And why? Some years before, George Gershwin died at 39 with a brain tumor in the frontal area that correlated sound and music, just as though that area had been overused. And the impression stuck, to the point that subconsciously I could see myself overusing part of my brain to the point of neoplasm. It was a fantasy, of course. I called Dr. John Adams, neurosurgical professor and tennis mate at Cal, to see if I should see him. He laughed, saying he would order skull films if I insisted. I thus learned that stress and the imagination make great bedfellows. The "brain tumor" did not appear. So I continued to think aggressively, thankful I could do so.

Frank Lind, and Dr. Southey and his "tubes"

I was called to Merritt Hospital by internist Ed Blaisdell to see his father-in-law, in acute trouble from a sudden hypertension of over 300 mm. systolic, which quickly could be fatal to a man in his sixties or older. My IVP (kidney X-ray) showed a smaller right kidney and barely adequate total kidney function. I was proficient with kidney function measurements, which included tests of relative excretion of sodium, chloride, and potassium—a study neglected by most at the time—but no facts could be left out of my Process Mind checklist. I proved that the smaller right kidney had a damaged blood supply causing the blood pressure. The small kidney had to be removed, and promptly.

I did a rapid surgery through the anterior incision. His pressure started to fall while still in surgery. My experience in Boston then paid off as I started a vasoconstrictor, Neo-synephrine, to hold closed the blood vessels and thus keep the systolic pressure up at 160. He was out of danger, as we allowed time for the circulatory system to adjust and settle down. In the ward, we waited for a few days before decreasing the dosage to zero, while his systolic remained steadily in the 140s. It was safe then to send him home.

Frank was well for a year. Then I was called again, because he had another sudden rise to over 300 mm., and it looked like the jig was up. Again, my Boston experience paid off, as I started Apresoline, a vasodilator, bringing his systolic down to 160 mm. It was held there for several days. We then weaned him off the medication slowly to the point that he stabilized at or below 160, never to rise again. Obviously, some sort of reflex arc involving the sympathetic nervous system had been broken. Boston with Dr. Smithwick echoed.

Then, things got more interesting. Once the pressure was controlled, he started to retain fluid, some 40 pounds worth, with massively swollen legs, as though in heart failure, but that was not the diagnosis. He also had become resistant to the diuretic effect of Mercuhydrin. It was the only diuretic available then, and it failed. What was I to do?

I remembered Dr. Addis telling me about Dr. Southey, back in the 1800s, placing quills in the swollen legs of his patients, who we now know were in heart failure. He had drawn, should I say "dripped," away the extra fluids. This was akin to tapping maple syrup from the tree. I would give this a try.

I cut short "quills" from plastic IV tubing, sharpened them, and placed two in each upper calf. The flow started immediately, almost in spurts. Frank sat with his feet in a large metal wash basin. His legs shrank, while he continued to claim, "I am losing my muscles." Three days later, forty pounds and twenty liters lighter, now with normal legs, Frank was discharged home. From that day on the diuretic

Mercuhydrin was again effective as it removed excess body fluid. He lived another ten years in fine health before a heart attack took him away.

I had learned once again that a normal water-to-tissue ratio, so named by Marcus Krupp, is essential for physiologic actions to have the greatest chance to be effective. If fluid is in excess, cellular functions are damaged until the balance is restored. The ability of the diuretic Mercuhydrin to work, once the water-to-tissue ratio was normal, speaks for itself.

CHAPTER

12.

Pediatric Urology is Pioneered

My first pediatric challenges—hypospadias and testicular torsion

Donald Smith's training in hypospadias repair set the stage for me to begin my first foray into the new subspecialty of Pediatric Urology without even trying. The second lesion, also congenital, was torsion of the testicle. The envelope around the testicle, the *tunica vaginalis,* is normally attached in a way that holds the testis in position, acting like the dorsal fin of a fish. If the attachment is faulty, the testicle hangs as if it were a clapper in a bell, and is free to twist as much as 720 degrees. In so doing, blood supply is instantly cut off. Within three hours the testicle could be gangrenous and unsalvageable. The urologist must be always on call, rush to the operating room, and untwist the testicle, trying to save it. That was state of the art and the Standard of Care.

When called, I responded, always ready to go, no matter the inconvenience. Carol and my daughters understood the need. I began to spread the word to pediatricians and general practitioners. In two years, I had seen 14 children. I had also made a mistake that led to loss of a testicle, as I had accepted standard texts' claims that severe pain was the first symptom of torsion, placing swelling in second place. A painless swelling in a 6-year-old was observed too long, and my surgery was too late. This must not happen again. My credo, as implied by my mentor dad, was, "One mistake is allowed. A second same mistake is unacceptable."

Researching the literature, I was astounded that no case series was greater than three, and nothing helpful was offered. To have 14 cases demanded action and pertinent observations, and I had several new items to offer. On six occasions, after I gained the child's confidence, I was able to inject one cc. of Novocain into the spermatic cord, making the testicle painless, and I could immediately manipulate it back to normal. In each instance the testicle was saved because I didn't follow the Standard of Care, which demanded I rush to the operating room, expose the testis under anaesthesia and then manipulate it. This "emergency" sequence delays detorsion for up to three more hours, and can only increase the danger of gangrene. The value of the cord block cannot be overestimated.

My next recommendation was to make swelling the prime diagnosis and not count on pain at all. Swelling alone was quite enough. I had found that the younger the child, the less the pain. Dr. Hinman had warned that the anomaly could be present on both sides. To make sure a viable testis is left, the opposite testis must always be sutured in place (orchiopexy), never allowed to twist.

Our cases were convincing, for half the time a similar anomaly prone to twist, or "torse," was found with the opposite testis. This demand raised the specter of malpractice suits. I was creating a new Standard of Care. I had no hesitation to decide that testis salvage was the issue, and it was time to "do it now." Bilateral exploration and orchiopexies must be mandatory. I hoped for immediate acceptance.

The report appeared in 1964, not in a urological journal, but in the Journal of the American Medical Association. The word needed to be spread abroad to all physicians, not just urologists and pediatricians. The problems were clear. The solutions were equally clear. Was I effective? The answer is yes, in one respect: since that day, bilateral orchiopexy is The Standard of Care. Would the diagnosis now be based on just acute swelling of the scrotum with or without pain? I hope this admonition took.

The use of spermatic cord anaesthesia, however, was entirely overlooked for another 30 years. How could this be? I learned a lesson: the compilers of new editions of teaching texts, which are mostly repetitious, usually just transfer the existing reference list without searching out the latest contributions. The spermatic cord block went unnoticed. Thus, many salvageable testes were likely lost. Testifying in a court case in Fairfax County near Washington, D.C., a few years ago, although I'm retired, my defense of a urologist using the block was successful. As a result, the court decided that two Standards of Care exist, with the cord block not required in the large teaching institutions where a trip to the operating room was more practical, no matter the price.

As I examine my actions, I recognize that the lifetime habit of keeping records, then analyzing them as taught me by Dad, with his graphs of trends, was already in place. Particularly valuable turned out to be my crude drawings on every operative note, something Uncle Bert had advised me to do.

Acute epididymitis re-visited

Infiltration of the spermatic cord with an anaesthetic to allow prompt reduction of a testicular torsion had two roots. The first was my experience in Boston, where infiltration of the lumbar sympathetic nerves was frequently required. The second was my urological mentor, Dr. Donald Smith, who had effectively employed the cord block for acute epididymitis, where massive painful swelling of the epididymis usually lasted as long as three weeks, despite antibiotics, local heat, and bed rest. Its cause remains unclear, even today. The cord block, more than half the time, resulted in immediate and continued pain control, and a return to a normal scrotum within 72 hours. Instead of weeks off the job, the patient is back to work within days. My experience with the spermatic cord block was just as dramatic. I have considered it a great gift and wondered why others do not know of its existence. An explanation of its action is needed.

I have mentioned Hans Selye, now immortal for his recognition of the sympathetic nervous system and its actions as instigator of the alarm reaction. This nervous system has been inherited from the animal, where survival demanded that blood loss be stanched. These fragile nerves are able to constrict the blood vessels, so that clotting can occur and a life be saved, but there is a price, for with injury or inflammation, the lack of oxygenated blood necessary for the healing process is delayed. The spermatic cord block therefore accomplishes two goals—the somatic nerves that transmit pain are blocked, and scrotal contents can be sensitively palpated. At the same time, the sympathetic nerves are blocked, thus allowing the blood vessels to open and, with their oxygen, healing immediately begins, manifested by rapid loss of swelling (edema).

Google today lists treatments that include bed rest, heat applications, and elevation of the scrotum. Nothing has changed in the 65 years since Donald Smith reported his experience in the 1943 Journal of Urology. I am compelled to try and remedy this oversight by educating both patient and physician. This is the sequence of my learning.

Henry Bruyn, chief of epidemiology on the UC service at San Francisco's County Hospital, was studying mumps and its painful complication, a melon-sized swelling of the scrotum known as epididymo-orchitis. He wished to study the fluid that filled the scrotum. Could I obtain some for him?

I faced a truly miserable patient with a fever of 105 degrees. In order to make my needle painless, I injected both spermatic cords with Novocain. Under complete scrotal anaesthesia, I then probed and recovered the desired fluid. The next day, Henry called to say, "I think you had better come see your patient." He made no further comment. My reaction was, "What have I done wrong?"

I rushed over, to find a smiling man, fever having dropped to normal overnight, with a scrotum no longer painful and well on its way to normalcy. The spermatic cord block had worked again.

That was my first encounter with the scrotal manifestation of mumps. The second came in private practice, when a young, vigorous professional bike rider came into the office, he too with a high fever, and a painful swollen scrotum. In Phoenix, he had been given antibiotics that were not effective. Their diagnosis was acute epididymitis. It was the fever that alerted me, and I took some blood to the lab, asking for a mumps-titer. Ten days later, this diagnosis was confirmed.

I promptly injected the spermatic cord, for whatever the origin of the epididymitis, the treatment would be the same. I carefully palpated the scrotal contents and ruled out a torsion, while at the same time he was receiving my standard treatment for acute epididymitis. The next day he was pain-free, without fever, and his scrotal swelling was resolving. He promptly went back on the road to meet his training schedule.

In the mid-1960s, I was making rounds at Presbyterian Hospital in New York with the residents and their chief, Dr. Keith Waterhouse, who recently passed. He is a legend, for his inquiring mind—likely to be Process—never stopped searching for a better way to do things. I saw a patient sitting up in bed, his enlarged scrotum draped with hot poultices. It had to be a full blown acute epididymitis, the patient suitably miserable.

With Keith's assent, I said, "Please bring me a small syringe and some Xylocaine." I injected several cc's into the spermatic cord. I mentioned to the residents that the same injection in a patient with torsion would allow its immediate correction. In the mail, one week later, came a Polaroid photo of this patient with a broad smile as he left the hospital. Keith Waterhouse made sure that the value and technique of spermatic cord block was taught each resident through the years. It was such a resident who led to my appearing in court in his behalf when he had attempted by cord block to save a testicle and was able to immediately reduce the torsion.

Busy days

Our Berkeley home was a four-story stucco Victorian building with a tennis court, a bit small, but great for a neighborhood playground. It was built by "Hungry Peterson" to house his eight children, somehow sired between long trips to and from the Arctic in his four-masted merchantmen. The house was like the inside of his ships, walled with dark mahogany, and the upstairs family room was a small replica of a ship's forecastle. The many stairs kept Carol in shape, and each of the three girls had her own room.

I had maintained close ties to Donald Smith, UC urology department chief, when he did a strange thing. He cancelled his urology classes, assigning their 20 hours to me to teach fluid-electrolyte balance to third-year students as a new subject in the curriculum. Over two years I had these hours with all of the third year students. A syllabus was required, and somehow, in the wee small hours of the night, I completed it. We sent it east for possible publication, but it was summarily turned down: it was just too "simple" when judged by the "experts," a problem I have met many times and never overcome. My students seemed to lap up this uncomplicated approach, particularly when one of the insufferably smart students would take me on, to be demolished as I let him shoot himself in the foot as his own ignorance of the subject was exposed.

Now I look back in awe. Where did the time and energy come from to combine this activity with private practice and home life? I have since concluded that it was made possible by the energy created by enthusiasm. Others might call it passion. Nevertheless, for the next years, the trips across the Bay were many as I taught students and, at times, operated on a patient with a special problem. These surgical episodes were not to my liking, because I couldn't be at hand every moment, and had to count on residents to do the right things. I never overcame the fear that I might not be there when needed. How wonderful in Berkeley to be minutes away from every patient.

Distal Urethral Stenosis—the "Irritating" Distal Urethral Ring

As the pediatric practice grew, I was almost overwhelmed with little girls who seemed miserable with their voiding difficulties and wet underwear. When an infection was not found, the problem appeared insurmountable as pediatricians and psychologists gave up, placing these youngsters at my door. The problem spoke for itself. I must search for a solution.

Why not start at the beginning and have the girls show me what the problem was, for a child's ability to list symptoms beyond saying,

"My bottom hurts" or "My tummy hurts" is not much help. Why not study their flows. What better way to do it than in the isolation of the bathroom, there to record their flows on a tape recorder? In academia, others were placing catheters in frightened children and measuring pressures in bladder and urethras, a true representation of what was really going on quite impossible. Fear and discomfort would deform any finding. I would, in my way, keep things simple, comfortable, and unobtrusive. A potty hanging in the toilet, its sounds dulled by the plastic, proved ideal. Thus was born the Piddle Patterns that the name Lyon would be associated with as the years went by. How often has someone said, "Oh, you're the Piddle Pattern Man." If that had a demeaning intent, I took it otherwise. It's good to be remembered one day with a smile.

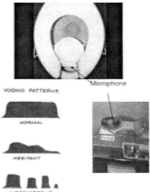

The recorder piled up roll after roll of tape, and I listened over and over and over again. Eventually, I could recognize just three distinct patterns of voiding. One, the Normal, was so rare in practice that I had to depend on my three daughters for examples. The force of flow varied, but the smooth pattern without terminal dribbling was unmistakable. Later, to test this belief, on a Labor Day weekend, we had cookies and drinks for the little girls in our neighborhood, who happily made piddle patterns in the seclusion of the bathroom. Low and behold these were all Normal too, confirming my hope that the recordings were valid, and thus the children heard in my office with other patterns definitely had serious problems.

The Hesitant pattern was the rule for those girls with tummy aches, damp underwear, irritated perineums, and just downright unhappy, disturbed personalities. The Hesitant has a slow start, as if by straining, with a continuous irregular flow, always with a slow finish and terminal dribbling, and this flow did not vary when repeated.

The third and final pattern I termed Intermittent, for it is a series of sharp starts and stops, almost squirts, as if the bladder was fighting a series of involuntary sphincter muscle contractions. If I would then check for urine left behind (the residual) there was always enough urine left in the bladder to invite infections, unlike the Hesitant streamers. These children would be my most difficult challenges, for infections were persistent. Fortunately, there were just a few.

Would voiding-cystourethragrams (X-rays of dye-filled bladders), something I was able to achieve consistently at cystoscopy time, be a help diagnostically? Our Hospital anesthesiologists were probably the best in the world. They could provide light enough anaesthesia that would allow voiding. It would be done as anaesthesia was induced. There were four urethral outlines, all with terminal narrowing, but nothing diagnostic, save the rare one demonstrating a thin line as the muscle went into severe spasm even during anaesthesia. The voiding-urethragram was of value in one respect. It was obvious that the child's urethra itself was large enough, almost adult size, that it would not be stretched by a large endoscope, and yet I was bothered by not recognizing something that was causing the difficult urination.

When I correlated signs, symptoms, voiding patterns and infections on my multi-columned spread sheets, it was time to report on this form of urodynamics as a diagnostic reality. I went south to the newly-appearing Pediatric Society urology meetings. I was sure that the presentation would elicit every kind of reaction from laughter to disbelief. Sure enough, the titters began when I identified my daughters' streams as the Normals, to follow with the Hesitant and Intermittent examples. I was prepared for instant derision. I must not react. It was just not taken seriously by the many. However, as I left at the meeting's end, two professors of urology stopped me to say, "Dick, keep it up. You've got something." The first was John Lattimer from New York, and the second, Willard Goodwin of UCLA. Their agile open minds had made them "giants." Did their encouragement make a difference? Yes, for they confirmed something I was going to pursue anyway. Was I effective? I guess so, if being the Piddle Pattern Man is an indicator of success, yet not the only success I would have wished.

Now this story takes a new twist. Fate, or serendipity, then stepped in the door. Some years before, surgeon Sumner Evringham had presented me with a handsome leather-bound box containing silver Bougies à Boulé. The box had been on my  desk for months as I wondered how they could be useful. The bougies looked like turnips of different sizes, each at the end of a thin rod. They were made in France to be used to locate scars (strictures) in the male urethra caused by the venereal disease gonorrhea. I kept wondering if I could find some use for them.

Dr. Brad Young in San Francisco believed the girls' voiding problems, often leading to infections, were the result of a tight and thick bladder neck. He advocated doing a YV plasty, the same operation I had introduced while a resident, for the closed bladder neck of my first adult patient with a posterior urethral valve. Why not take these bougies, pass them through the urethra into the bladder, and see if, by feel, I could verify that the bladder neck was truly thick?

Surprise! Only the smallest bougie would pass all of the way to the bladder. The next larger size snapped through something just within the urethral opening (meatus). This "something" felt like a thin membrane, much like the pre-pubertal hymen. I turned to the anatomy texts. No such structure was described. It would have to be called a discovery. The next step one would term an adventure. It was logical to believe this membrane was obstrucing flow. I applied Bernoulli's theorem relating flow to orifice size and pressure. The smallest opening in the membrane allowed a normal flow. Something else was producing the Hesitant and Intermittent streams. It had to be the muscular urethra, contracting in response to the irritation the membrane must be causing.

It was then that I recalled mentor John Schulte had reported a striking case of a little girl whose symptoms were those I have just described. He had dilated her urethra aggressively, supposing that the scarring by a stricture was the problem. She was cured! Had John used the bougies given me, he would have made the same discovery years earlier. The membrane must be inactivated.

With my patient anesthetized, I started with an F 10 sound (cigar-shaped metal dilator), noticed resistance with an F 16, F 18, F 20, F 22. With F 24, something gave way! F 26 and F 28, then unresisted, fell in. The membrane had split at F 24. A drop of blood appeared; the job was done.

Until the next office visit a week later, I was on my guard. No phone calls, so I guessed things must be okay. On her first visit, only a few days later, my little patient ran down the hall toward me asking for "my cookie," a wide smile having displaced the concerned frown the week before. Her piddle pattern was now normal! I knew the game was won. Mom was in tears of joy, because now she knew that she and her husband were not causing the problem.

What was I to call this membrane that acted as an irritant, its lumen almost never so small that a normal flow could not occur. It wasn't obstructive. The urethral muscle above must be the constricting agent. I believed it was involuntary and responding to the irritation of the Ring membrane as it narrowed the flow, much as an anal fissure would produce string stools. Its consistency and location suggested

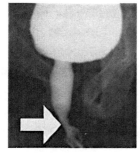

DISTAL URETHRAL RING

similarity to the pre-pubertal hymen which softens at puberty. I named the membrane the *Distal Urethral Ring*—the syndrome, *Distal Urethral Stenosis*. The membrane is likely to soften and perhaps disappear at puberty, but by then the psychological impact remains, as some women are bothered by a nagging urgency and frequency through later years.

One thousand unhappy little girls had their Ring membranes broken. In only a few was an immediate dramatic change not the rule. Teachers called parents to find out what had happened, for their students had stopped fidgeting, seemed no longer preoccupied, and stopped suddenly running to the bathroom. Grades sky-rocketed as attention spans became normal. Constipation disappeared. Even tiny tots could be fed, as they had stopped fidgeting. One would think that the problem was solved, yet being effective was another matter.

Today the procedure is known, and yet used only by a few, and they may be under pressure for the reasons I will describe. To me it is a monstrous mistake, as it denies quick, effective treatment on a spurious basis. I will explain.

The decade following the publication of my findings and results was marked by ready acceptance, with some 20 papers reporting similar results, emphasizing remarkable rates of infection cure. There were always a few who, perhaps seeking prominence, took a negative view. They claimed the Distal Urethral Ring was not obstructive. It never was claimed to be obstructive! Clearly, the critics had chosen not to seriously study the report and thus, perhaps playing politics, diverted the issue.

Distal Urethral Stenosis at 21

In the operating room I was preparing for the simple process of inactivating a Distal Urethral Ring membrane in another little girl, miserable with her mysterious problem. The X-ray technician said, "Dr. Lyon. You tell these wonderful stories about what you are doing. Do you think you can help me?"

This was her tale: Her marriage was at risk because of a lifetime habit of having to void every hour day and night. To me this seemed unbelievable to have gone uncared for until now. I said, "Margaret, please come to my office, and I'll see if I can discover the problem."

With her urethra anaesthetized with Xylocaine, my Bougie à Boulé struck a resistant Ring just within the urethral opening (the meatus). Its caliber was a very small F 16, probably unchanged from girlhood. It had not softened with time. The caliber was large enough to allow for a normal flow, but its irritant effects seemed still to be in place. The endoscope disclosed a perfectly normal bladder, save for its small capacity of only 100 cc's. No wonder the urinary frequency, but was the small capacity bladder the cart or the horse?

To see someone with a persistent Ring in their twenties was a unique experience for me. I said, "Let's go for broke. Grit your teeth for a moment as I rupture the Ring." It gave way at F 26 in classic fashion, just as with the very young. Margaret came back in a week, smiles broader than ever. "I sleep all night and go to the bathroom two or three times a day. Thank you so much."

Her bladder capacity had, within the week, increased to a normal 300 cc's. The Ring was obviously the horse, and the bladder the cart. My beliefs about the Ring as just being an irritant setting off the urge to void was again confirmed.

The story should end here, but several months later Margaret appeared with a bladder infection, clearly after intercourse. I said, "Margaret now that you are like the rest of us, you must drink two big glasses of water after each intercourse so that your now normal bladder, filling up rapidly, will awaken you before the bacteria can multiply, and will flush out the critters." She did that and lived happily ever after, I am told.

Without my trusty bougies to identify the Distal Urethral Ring membrane, I would have tried a urethral dilatation, as John Schulte did in the manner used so successfully for adults. I would never have known that it was just a Distal Urethral Ring that gave way. Over the years, I discovered, with the bougies, over 20 adults with Rings still intact who responded to the single dilatation. However, with urgency and frequency habitually in place, they never quite duplicated the success of Margaret.

Professors of pediatric urology are created in America

An unexpected transition occurred as Pediatric Urology was being pushed as a separate specialty by those in the residency programs who did not share the view of the older, experienced urologists. We believed that, by extending standard procedures to the very young, we were just broadening the specialty field. Everyone agreed that a year in England at St. Ormond Street Hospital for Children in London would be valuable, for the number of patients seen in this institution is enormous. Yet, something was amiss. It was true that all of the pediatric procedures our American Fellows would witness in England were of American origin. However, I was told that discussion of therapy directed at the little girls' urethras had not occurred. It seemed to be a "no-no." Was the treatment so uncomplicated that it was not worth discussing?

I spent two days as an observer. In the clinic we saw some sad cases of neglect, and many with acute needs. On my first day there, a 9-year-old came in with the signs and symptoms of DUS, a mild complaint compared to those I had just seen. She was promptly scheduled for the operating room the next day. I was astounded and said to the clinician, "Isn't this problem too minor to be a competitor for operating time. What will you do?"

"I will take a look."

"And see what?"

"I'll see something."

"Will you use your largest scope, for instance, an F 26?"

"Yes." It seemed obvious that the large endoscope would break the Ring membrane, with his observers none the wiser.

The new cadre of professors-to-be came home thoroughly convinced that the DUS syndrome was a hoax. They returned to pills, invasive urodynamics tests, and psychological help. It is the same today, forty years later. Can I do something about this? I am still trying, for the conscientious pediatric urologist is missing each day the joy of being effective.

CHAPTER

13.
The Changing World

My practice grows; I tire; I gain a partner

It would seem I had quite enough on my platter, but each day brought with it something else that had to be considered in the mix that was beginning to take place. The three girls were growing up. I was still practicing solo. Our summer vacations, riding the waves in La Jolla and Del Mar lengthened, as I found practice fatigue expressing itself in the number of weeks it would take for me to relax and become sleepy during the day. First, it was one week, then two, then three. When it reached four, I got the message and looked for a partner. My first choice failed to meet my criteria for honesty. That association lasted just a year, as I became wary of my ability to judge people. I practiced by myself for another three years.

Don Smith again proved a savior when he sent Sumner Marshall as ideal for the job. Sumner and I were a match, and though we later had several other partners come and go, Sumner and I were simpatico to the day I retired, leaving him to then carry on our traditions.

I do my part in a changing Berkeley world, with home and family taking precedence

The most pressing problem was to recognize the changes taking place in this Athens of the West. Our first decade in Berkeley was as we expected it would be. Alta Bates Hospital was possibly the finest in the world, for its nurses were incomparable, and its medical staff immensely talented men who turned down enticing academic careers, and who, like me, loved the well-rounded life Berkeley offered.

135

Weather, of course, played its part. There was no mediocre medicine or surgery at Alta Bates, and my innovative forays were accepted and encouraged. In other words, ambition and envy simply did not exist, and the pathology and radiology departments were second to none, led by physicians who shared their pride.

The first step away from "Athens" was suggested to me a number of years ago by Dr. John Saunders, the accomplished anatomist at UC Berkeley. He had become Chancellor of the University for just long enough to assure the resignation of President Clark Kerr, who seemed not to understand the UC Berkeley conflicts. Dr. Saunders told me that in the late 1950s he sensed the changes to come when he noticed that the city no longer enforced ordinances related to housing. The doors were thus opened for the outside to move in, and live not as families but as communes.

Then the UC bandwagon appeared, subtly at first, as civil servants and university professors moved in from the outside, primarily from New York City. They knew that they were joining an academic world of immense acceptance and tolerance, and that they could direct change in such an uncritical atmosphere. Two years later, I accosted such a professor who was leaving to return to New York because, he said, "I can't get my children educated." What a change from the school system my oldest daughter, Kathy, had known, and my two younger daughters, Joan and Laura, were just recognizing as failing.

Politics had entered in the form of busing students when Neil Sullivan came to Berkeley from New England, courtesy of a progressive school board. He would take over the schools as superintendent with the apparent intent to have busing in place by presidential election time. I believe that this was the first major busing program in the country. I was so concerned about the $600,000 to be diverted from such uses as more and smaller classes in the black neighborhoods, that I presented my feelings to the School Board in the high school auditorium. Black and white citizens filled the room. I criticized the whole busing concept as counterproductive to a remarkable education program already in place. My comments were received with loud applause. Perhaps I knew my community better than most.

At that time, Berkeley must have been leading the nation in its devotion to educational advances. Our first six grades in the black neighborhoods were receiving the heaviest financial backing. With smaller classes, but, more importantly, with proximity to homes, parents came into the classrooms for direct participation. As I pointed out to new Superintendent Sullivan, this family involvement would end when a child is bused to far off parts of Berkeley, all for the sake of diversity. Parents could no longer be close at hand. Nevertheless, busing was implemented. With the passing of Robert Kennedy, the next January found Mr. Sullivan back in Massachusetts at some promised job, leaving us with this misadventure from which our city never recovered.

Before Mr. Sullivan, geography dictated that schools serve their neighborhoods. The first six grades seemed segregated, but the reward was closeness to home and family participation. This appeared to be a racial separation. The fact is that this separation was primarily on an economic basis. Once the children reached the seventh grade, they came together, fully prepared to compete as ethnic lines blurred. The diverse population at Willard Junior High School on Telegraph Avenue and at Berkeley High School was a joy to behold, as well as be a participant. Ethnic lines gave way to social and cultural capabilities. My girls felt perfectly at home in the schoolroom or at the school proms.

Then the political system got further into the act. Here was democracy being grossly misused by the few, and Berkeley was not worldly enough to recognize the invasion. Our unquestioning tolerance, always a danger in a free culture, did not recognize the discipline that democracy requires to survive.

I invited a dozen or so citizens to have breakfast at the hospital on each Wednesday. In a few months, the result was the creation of a working group known as Concerned Berkeley Citizens (CBC). It knew no party lines. This group functioned for the next three years, interviewing candidates for the City Council and then acting to elect their choices. I believe I was the only registered Republican in the group, though the larger group to follow may have had a few, such as General William Dean, famed as a prisoner for his years of survival in solitary confinement in Korea.

The election of 1966 followed our hopes, and the election of 1968 seemed to be on the same track. All of the chosen candidates represented a broad base from liberal to moderate. Our candidate, Bill Sweeney, highly respected judge of Afro-American heritage, seemed destined to be the next mayor. Suddenly, out of the blue appeared John DeBonis, a blustering past-councilman with solid backing from a group known as the BCU—Berkeley Citizens United—a long-time, semi-active group made up of 5,000 older citizens, who, on the surface, would seem to be ultraconservative. My protestations to them that their 5,000 votes would doom our more moderate approach reached deaf ears, and the result was a loss to a progressive candidate by only 2,000 votes. Thus, the critical turn was not accomplished by an advancing liberal agenda, but by a shortsighted older Berkeley citizenry who wouldn't believe what was happening as democracy was subverted.

At the same time, I had adopted another line of direct action. Some forty business and professional citizens came to my home to see what could be done. The result was that all agreed to my request for participation, the only way left with a hope of being effective. All agreed to attend monthly city council meetings for one year. Twenty did. As it turned out, this didn't work either. Perhaps there is an explanation as to why.

The young rebels, the "Chicago Seven," showed up in Berkeley, having traveled from Columbia to Michigan State and to UC Berkeley, as the airplane made them seem to be everywhere. The result was that we Berkeley citizens were ineffective, with student discontent raging and threatening the serenity we prized, which was quickly lost. How, in a major city, could this happen?

We were sitting ducks, with great ideals, generosity supported by beliefs that took democracy for granted, but this inertia of apparent success made us vulnerable to the small groups that would subvert these ideals.

There was a second contribution. A city the size of Berkeley usually has leaders of industry who also are leaders in public life. Berkeley had such potential leaders, but they considered Berkeley just a delightful place to live. Their offices were in San Francisco, and there they exerted their leadership. This absence of direction was a telling blow.

Governor Reagan rescues Berkeley for a moment

When things were at their worst, after a physical confrontation on Telegraph Avenue between angry students and the Sheriff's Department, I was crossing Shattuck Avenue and ran into Police Chief Biehl. I had met with him each Friday for months to try to be supportive. He was ashen. I asked if he was going to have a heart attack or perforate an ulcer. He said that he had reason to, because "Telegraph Avenue is about to blow," gunfire and all, and he hadn't been able to get help from the State. I said, "See you later," and went to the pay phone nearby. It was Friday afternoon when public officials often had left for the weekend. I put in my nickel, and by sheer good fortune found Don Mulford, our state representative in the office and on the phone. I said, "Don, if you don't get Governor Reagan to do something, Berkeley will blow up, and you will be to blame." Click! In force, the State Highway Patrol sped by me on Shattuck Avenue ten minutes later. The city remained quiet. Again it was great to be effective.

The Gerwick-Lyon-Nixon story.

This next account has particular reference to my attempts to reach Bill Gates with an equally far-out idea and again met failure. The value of telling this story is to emphasize how little things may effect change over time, as long as one is persistent. These next two adventures occurred forty years apart.

In the year that John Kennedy and Richard Nixon were sparring, I talked with engineer Ben Gerwick, a pioneer in underwater construction, about what America might do at the world level. Our basic agreement led to a letter, two pages in length, that we composed on a Sunday evening at the Berkeley Tennis Club.

We both believed at that time that America was searching for a way to spread its largess into the undeveloped world. We focused on South America. As I look back, it was a barometer of the world and its shrinkage, because the Middle East was not considered. We envisioned sending teams of experienced experts to any country wishing to solve a specific problem, such as education in a town. Ben and I saw this as complex, for an efficient school needs more than four walls and a teacher. It requires pure water, sanitation, sewage disposal, etc. Our teams were to be the heads of successful organizations, willing to do this in close-knit groups. As a starter, it would involve a two-year assignment, and payment would be on the same scale as received in their own businesses.

We placed our letter in the pocket of Stan McCaffery, a right-hand man to Nixon, and a close friend of ours. We expected him to give it to Mr. Nixon on his visit to California, but nothing happened. Oddly, we never complained to Stan about this because the next time we saw each other it was too late, and why demand an excuse?

In September of that year, I believe, the Youth Corps concept was adopted by John Kennedy. When I went to the hospital, friends stopped me to say that our plan had been purloined. My answer was that this was not the case, and the new plan had to come from somewhere else. I also felt it inadequate, for it placed amateurs in positions requiring pros. At the same time, it would have immense appeal to the young electorate and would give American youths a great experience. The election hung on a few votes. I have always believed the Youth Corps made the difference.

The next January, a young man named Bill came into my office with a refractory ailment picked up in South America. Could I cure it? Yes, and it was not difficult to do. When I asked him what he had been doing there, he said, "Fore-running the Peace Corps." I showed him our plan, and he had to smile, for their original plan was much like ours. When I asked who financed the project, he said, "Mr. Watson of IBM." I knew that Mr. Watson had voted as a Democrat, although he was known as a staunch Republican. My next question was, "Didn't

Mr. Watson give this to Mr. Nixon first?" The answer was, "Yes, but Nixon turned it down."

That was in June, I suspect before our proposal arrived, and Stan had believed it to be a lost cause. The final note is that Bill became head of the Youth Corps later, so this tale hangs beautifully together.

I wonder how different things might be now, if Richard Nixon had possessed the imagination and vision of John Kennedy?

I try again, this time for Iraq

Mr. President:

First, may I introduce myself. I am a retired urologist who, as president of the Napa World Affairs Council some years ago, with my wife Carol was privileged to have Dr. Condoleezza Rice as our dinner guest. We knew then that Dr. Rice was on her way into American history, and now you are so fortunate to have the vision to have her at your side. For three years, on the Internet, I have been mentoring pediatric surgeons in Pakistan, India, and Rumania, teaching them the processes of urology. They must care for all children, regardless of diagnosis, in a struggling world of such poverty we cannot imagine. And thus, I see America's mission as so much broader than providing sustenance and safety, with the stability of education being the greatest need. So, I have a thought.

In Iraq, as well as in all of the Middle Eastern countries, the present and the future lies in the hands of the young—those now wielding instruments of death. Yet, these angry feelings could give way quickly to a feeling of personal worth. Can we do something about this? Though my belief is exotic and on the surface unachievable, the message remains the same. I tried to reach Steve Jobs, for I remember his foray with the Apple into the schools, surely expensive at the moment, but a stimulus to the communication world he was helping to build. So, my thought is this. If a computer, whether by Apple, Compact, Dell, or the Gates Foundation, as an American venture, were to find its way into each Iraqi schoolroom, not tomorrow, but now, as things hang on a knife edge, a healing process would be in place. Some object with, "but Iraqis don't speak English." My answer is, "Put the kids' Fedayeen-fingers on a computer keyboard connecting with a new friend in America, and those boys will be computer fluent in word-processed English in a matter of weeks to a few months. Their guns will rust." What makes this venture so inviting is that computers will malfunction or be broken, while available to every classroom will be a young American GI, fluent in computerese and maintenance, and anxious to help.

Yours truly,
Richards Lyon, MD

That was my message. I expected it not to be taken seriously, but I felt I must try. It was 2003, and I was anxious to push this concept hard, hoping to break through and make it not only a truly wondrous human step, but one with political implications. Again, I failed, despite almost a year of following up by letter, phone, and e-mail, every possible lead, which included industrial and government leaders of both political parties. I heard not a word until a single note came from the White House with just "Thanks."

If you believe in it, go for it. If it doesn't work, you've tried and tried, like the Puffer Billy, and it may eventually be effective without your knowing it.

Levity in a serious life—the asparagus fiasco

I have always been fascinated by the odor of asparagus (aspergine) in urine within an hour of its ingestion. What a wonderful home-test of kidney function, but the idea had never been taken seriously. I received a call from Oakland's Highland Hospital. They had a kidney shutdown in a patient who had ingested carbon tetrachloride, available in fire extinguishers, in a suicide attempt. Could I help?

I knew that the kidney insult was an acute tubular necrosis, as with a TUR, and that recovery was likely, if given ten days of careful fluid control. It also occurred to me that this was an opportunity to study asparagus as a practical kidney test. I went to Oakland to my friend

Tiger Hunt's food supply company. He gave me several cases of canned asparagus. I delivered them to the hospital, and asked my resident to feed our patient asparagus every day and to call me when the odor appeared. We would then apply proven tests for comparison.

This sounded pretty foolproof to me, but three weeks went by and no call. I reached the resident on the phone and asked what had happened. There was dead silence before he said, "I hate to tell you this, but we asked the patient the question for three weeks, and his answer was always 'No.' Finally, he volunteered that he had lost his sense of smell many years ago. I wish I had made the resident take a whiff each day as urine flow began, but the time advantage had been lost, and another great experimental observation denied for want of the imaginative right question. I was not effective, it seems.

Several weeks earlier, internist Gale Whiting had called to tell me about his patient who wondered that his very adequate urine flow looked like water and his asparagus intake brought no smell. Six days earlier his large artery, the aorta, had been studied with an aortogram (dye visible by X-ray), a test notorious for causing renal shutdown. I recognized this as a high-output kidney failure (LNN), to fully recover after ten days. Because urine output was normal, although quality abnormal, I decided it best to "let sleeping dogs lie." So, I couldn't follow through, although now I think I should have repeated the asparagus routine. Yes, lawyers were snooping around in those days, making unnecessary and nonproductive trouble. Someone will eventually make a name for himself with what would seem to be a humorous study—the odor of asparagus as a kidney test. There is still so much like this to do in our search for knowledge that requires just common sense, and a "Do it now" habit.

UC Bear Juice—before Gatorade

In the early 1960s, Jerry Patmont, team physician at UC Berkeley, asked if I could help in combating the cramps experienced by the football team when playing the University of Arkansas in the heat of the late summer. I asked Dr. John Saunders, friend, brilliant original thinker, and world traveler, as well as a professor of anatomy at the university, what Red Sea sailors used to combat dehydration. We reached agreement that a solution with 2 grams of salt per liter (estimated basal concentration in sweat) and 5% sugar for taste would prove a very palatable liquid. When consumed at about 1 liter every 30 minutes, it should do the job, and I would have salty potato chips everywhere.

It worked and is used to this day. Arkansas lost to California for the first time. We called it Bear Juice. I suggested to Jerry that he find a UC bottler and market this replacement solution to make money for Cal sports. When Jerry did nothing, I learned another lesson. If you have an original idea, you, and only you, must carry it forward or it is likely not to be realized.

I am sorry I didn't go ahead with this on my own, although I had plenty to do. The irony is that about two years later, Gatorade, an almost exact duplicate with a little unneeded potassium, was designed by a urologist in Florida. I have always wondered if he knew his fluid balance.

Ideas are rarely the domain of a single individual, for knowledge and mechanisms to utilize this knowledge abound, if one just looks. The designer of Gatorade recognized the problem. It didn't require an expert to solve it. It took common sense and a few paragraphs in a physiology text about the makeup of sweat.

Cine recordings and serendipity; ureteral orifice configuration and competence

The camera has played a major part in my life. Its most powerful effect has been on the quality of recall that brings with it exquisite memories of family life. In practice, I also used the camera to record what was in view, not with the intention of proving anything, but with the hope that this recall would reveal truths not otherwise possible to recognize in an instant of vision. This latter hope has been fully justified. The best examples are the recordings of the interior of the child's bladder, as I did my diagnostic cystoscopies. A few minutes were added to operating times, and I made sure they were well used.

I took no pictures until fiber optic lighting appeared in the late 1950s. All of a sudden, this constant light made photographic reproduction a reality via small instruments. By trial and error, I hit the perfect combination for true representation of what my eye saw. Though the fiber optic light seemed to mimic daylight, I discovered that Type A artificial light film, with this light from the new fiber optic source, produced normal mucus membrane colors. With my delicate, lightweight Beaulieu 16 mm. camera mounted on my small endoscope eye-piece, I recorded everything it revealed, to be studied later over and over again.

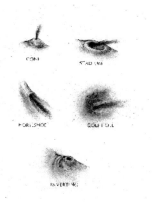

What made this experience in discovery unique? It was the recognition that orifices have four configurations that define their ability to act as one-way valves that do not allow bladder urine to be forced back into the kidneys, there to do immense damage. I named these Normal, Stadium, Horseshoe, and Golf Hole. They are congenital, structural variations that can direct the urologist as to the possibilities for success with medical or surgical intervention. My presentation won The Grand Prize for Clinical and Scientific Investigation at the American Urological Association meeting in 1968. This terminology is used today by experienced urologists. It is particularly valuable for the child.

Could these observations have been made without the repeated examination of films, later correlated with results? No, for the few minutes that I, the urologist, had had to look and judge orifices could never have resulted in anything more than just impressions. What a step forward was this! Urologists could now communicate through a conduit of understanding made possible by a terminology familiar to all. The camera, with its ability to return to a scene time and time again, is useless without the cameraman then spending hours looking, hoping to see something revealed—perhaps for the first time.

Cine in the operating room and a revelation

I would set the movie camera on a tripod, focused on my operating hands. My nurse turned it on and off as I worked. I would repeatedly review the films at home in the late evenings, striving to see what I had not recognized as I operated. The various grades of testicular damage were recorded on the many feet of film.

At one point, I noticed something for the first time. It had been there all along, of course, and it turned looking into seeing and recognizing. The normal epididymis, the tube carrying sperm from the testis, is attached to one side of the testicle, full 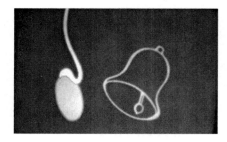 length, as with a fish's dorsal fin. However, on my films, the torsion-prone testicle is found to have its epididymis, attached always to the top of the testis where it connects with the testicle, becoming unattached and hanging free below. It can then curl up along the blood supply of the spermatic cord, leaving the testicle bare. In normal anatomy, the lower pole of the testis is covered by the epididymis, whereas the torsion-prone testicle with epididymis detached has a bare lower pole. This smoothness is easily palpated through the scrotal wall. Once this displacement of the epididymis is recognized as the anatomical defect, the "bell-clapper" designation is understood, and for the first time.

So, something was gained, although nothing changed in signs, symptoms, and treatment. The alert physician, by recognizing that the bare lower testicular pole discloses a testicle likely to twist, can anticipate the need for orchiopexy (testicle fixation) in the child before the event occurs. In the child or adult with intermittent unexplained scrotal aches, this physical finding can be diagnostic.

A year or so after the film study had been presented, a military group in Texas described this epididymis deformity without mentioning the observation in the film, so it may well be that this was a simultaneous confirmation. Yet today this observation remains unknown, as new texts don't include it and oversights persist.

In terms of defining The Problem, I get an A, based on the unique ability of cine to facilitate discovery. In terms of effectiveness, it is almost an F. I believe that the film never received the attention it deserved and has probably not been copied on video for the ACS library in the modern digital mode. I hope someone will rediscover it, if history is to be preserved.

Another breakthrough in fluid electrolyte balance— the recognition of insensible losses from the open abdomen

Dr. Henry Moorman came to Oakland as the first in a new breed, vascular surgeons, placing the local general surgeons on the defensive. He felt the pressure, for the kind of cases he would operate on would have wide influence on the surgical specialty. He asked me to help him as an assistant, because he wanted active, uncritical help, and also someone who knew something of fluid balance. I was his assistant with the first six cases, all aortic aneurysms (ballooning of the aorta that could rupture and be fatal). As a habitual routine, I carefully measured the fluid and electrolyte input-output backed up by body weights. Our very first case shut down, the kidneys in acute tubular necrosis fashion, as with a TUR.

I controlled his weight and prevented an overload. On the sixth day his kidney function returned. There was no hemolysis (abnormal breakdown of red cells), so this had to be the result of something else. My intake, output, and weight measurements provided the answer. He had lost 2 pounds, or 1000 cc's, of body salt and water for every one of the six hours we operated. So, this was clearly severe dehydration, probably its effects accentuated by the effects of not fully replaced blood losses.

At the time, this syndrome had been attributed to cross clamping of the aorta, compromising kidney blood flow during the repair. That explanation had never made sense to Henry or me, and the dehydration did. So, from that point on, every hour in the operating room—with an abdomen open and losing by evaporation its 6 grams of salt per liter of fluid—required immediate replacement by a combination of salt and water mimicking these losses. No further shut downs occurred. At the same time, I began to preach the gospel of the invisible, thus *insensible* fluid and salt losses of the open abdomen in surgery. I suspect that eventually someone else discovered these observations, too, for the problem appears to be solved.

This was a serendipitous discovery. It was the result of being in the right place at the right time and with the right homework already done.

The intake-output record becomes a hospital staple

Another fallout from my mission to bring sense into the system was the creation of Intake-Output sheets for the nursing records, first, in all of the East Bay hospitals, then extending to San Francisco at UCSF, and finally to the outlying cities. Body weight was becoming a daily requirement, a striking break with the past. What made this record unique was the insensible fluid loss, 800 cc's, included each day as output. I felt the need to defend my conception of mandatory insensible 800 cc losses. It took a few years to find the answer as to who originated the name and concept.

It was in Venice in those wonderfully productive years of Italian medical Renaissance of the early 1500s, where a nobleman named Sanctorius Sanctorius was fascinated by the relation of body weight and water. He was far ahead of his time—almost 400 years, installing primitive scales in his bathroom and elsewhere, he tracked his own daily weights against intake and measured visible output. 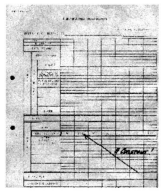 He found he always came up 800 cc's short. He recognized this for what it was, "invisible perspiration." He named it, *perspiratio insensibalis*.

So it is today. Incidentally, Sanctorius also invented the first practical thermometer. He was a Leonardo da Vinci of medicine. I wish I could have known him.

What I had learned, though, by this time is that anyone famous for just one discovery very likely took it from someone else, too busy to notice, or to really care. Sanctorius, the real creator, had discovered much more than just this, and entirely on his own.

Pioneering intermittent catheterization in children with meningomyelocoele

In the mid-1970s, Jack Lapides, professor at Michigan, told the American Association of GenitoUrinary Surgeons (AGUS), about two nurses who had resorted to self-catheterization when their bladder dysfunctions were so great that they could not void effectively. This was true serendipity, as Jack recognized the importance of this simple observation.

My thoughts were immediately directed to the many girls in our Birth Defects Clinic at Children's Hospital. I returned to give this a try. Fortunately, I was familiar with the glass curved-tip (coudé) catheters that Dr. Meads had used for years. I made these available to the parents. They found them easy to keep sterile and to re-use. It was simply a matter of teaching the technique. The idea took off.

That this worked and the girls stayed dry was the major step, but my habit of observing and recording all I could with my camera meant that again I had hundreds of feet of film. My habit of reviewing them over and over produced real dividends. I saw that orifice deformities subjected to the disorganized pull of the bladder muscles, typical of these neurogenic bladders, (no muscle-nerve balance) make for a high degree of seriously damaging reflux of urine into the kidneys as the orifices are pulled open when the bladder contracts. What the cines showed, along with collaborating X-rays, was that when the bladders were frequently emptied by catheterization, the aimless muscle-bundle spasms quieted down. The orifices, freed of these damaging "pulls" that dragged them open, became competent. This ended the need for corrective surgery, so fraught with difficulty by the original bladder-wall deformities. This revelation was totally unexpected. I am sure it would not have been noticed without the cines.

The article was published in the mid-1970s. It suffered for years the neglect that occurs by not being referenced in new texts. I have no problem with others receiving credit, but I do have a problem that the bladder changes leading to ureteral competence still are not recognized, or at the least, the mechanism of these positive changes still goes unnoticed while the need to know persists. But then again, we had a lot of happier children and parents from that first day. So, a major problem was solved. Thousands of girls, and adults too, are able to function without the social stigma their incontinence would otherwise create.

What a privilege to be effective, to sense the need and then be handed the cure just by being at the right place at the right time, and to know it!

Urinary diversion of boy with posterior urethral valve and relation to growth

Of all the observations I have stumbled on serendipitously, this ultimately may be the most important. Hormones that control body growth are still not fully understood, but the kidney is believed to be involved in this process. The observations that follow point to a growth factor having its origin in the cells of the kidney tubules. If this is the case, my experience with urinary diversion, which removes any possible obstruction to urinary flow, should provide insight. The boy with a posterior urethral valve (PUV) and obstruction to urine flow that is not entirely removed is small in stature. Once the obstruction is completely removed, the child rapidly achieves normal growth. It is likely that some type of growth hormone is the agent of this transformation.

The maximum obstructive urinary tract lesion compatible with life is the posterior urethral valve. From the moment of urine formation, the entire system is under intense hydraulic pressure, for the congenital lesion of valvular urethral stenosis (narrowing) must be transited for the urine to be evacuated. The boy is born with a thick, muscular bladder, tortuous inefficient ureters, often without muscle power, and hollowed-out kidneys with markedly diminished functioning parenchyma (kidney cells).

It is still generally accepted that destroying the valve and opening the lower tract is all that can be effective. At the start I, too, accepted this belief, but soon changed my mind when I realized that the baggy ureters were often functioning as tortuous, non-motile (inactive) conduits and acting as obstructions on their own. So, in the tradition of Frank Hinman, whose obstructive concepts were clear to those of us who trained with him, I took it upon myself to break the generally accepted rules, and interrupt the ureters in such a way that they would drain easily as straight conduits to a central single opening which would then be fitted with a bag, easy to change, and allowing the boy to go through prepubescent life without the wet pants of the other serious PUVs. Why are they uniformly wet? Because the damage to the kidney tubule is such that four times the fluid volume of normal is required to rid the body of each 24-hour's end products, and the child's efforts to keep up with the flow and stay dry is never perfect.

I had six boys with serious kidney damage already in place, with parents hoping that I could, by whatever means, improve the likely outcome. I therefore removed all chances of any continued obstruction to flow by interrupting the ureters as they entered the bladder, then bringing them together in a single stoma (opening to the outside) below the umbilicus, where a device could be fitted to collect the urine efficiently.

Before these six boys were diverted, I had another six who were less damaged, yet with very much the same ureteral limitations, and who were not diverted. In habitual fashion, all twelve boys were carefully followed, and what transpired blew me away. The undiverted six were all of small stature, in the 25th percentile or less, while the diverted six, although with greater renal damage, grew in the normal range, from fifty to one hundred percentile, averaging close to eighty. So there had to be a message. The badly damaged renal tubule, if it remains obstructed, must fail in the production of some growth factor normally produced by the cells of the unobstructed tubule.

My attempts to interest scientists and clinicians studying body growth and its factors have fallen on deaf ears. This is too bad, for time is awasting. Sooner or later, these findings will be made again, but I am astounded at the unwillingness of my young peers to open their eyes and minds to see the possibilities, let alone the value of full decompression for its other values beyond achieving normal stature. The diverted boys, all destined for eventual kidney failure, dialysis, and kidney transplants, were given many extra years of adequate kidney function. Because the diversion surgery was done close to birth, parents were spared many extra years of diapers and wet pants, while the boys accepted their appliances as normal. One boy, at age nine, won the state 50- and 100-yard dash championships for two years, his appliance not a hindrance.

CHAPTER
14.

At 65, Not Slowing Down, I Speed Up

Bondurant (Sears Point) Raceway

Giuseppe Cammaroto, friend and tennis pro at Silverado Country Club, knew of my not allowing myself the use of anything close to a sports car. I feared frequent brushes with the law as I drove home after a tiring day in surgery. I knew full well that my love of the automobile made us "one" on the road, and I would not notice that my speedometer registered 80 mph as my car would move so smoothly. He asked if I would like to take a spin in his Alfa Romeo Sports car. I did, driving it down a mountain road, most of the way under acceleration. Giuseppi, well tanned, was pale at the the end. It was obvious that my run was not what he had expected, nor had I.

I said, "Giuseppi, did I stay on my side of the road all of the way?" His answer: "Yes."

"Did I burn any rubber?"

"No."

However, he and I had learned something: if this was a built-in tendency of mine, as a fine car and I became one, I had better put myself in the hands of an expert to be sure I kept behaving safely as I aged. I was 65 years old and in the down stretch of life when I put the Alpha Romeo to the test. The message was clear.

So what could I do that I always had wanted to do, while still able to do it? Travel, fishing, scuba diving, body surfing, flying—all passed through my mind, but one exploit had won the day. The fine car was my Achilles heel, as the Alfa had proved. It was enrolling in the Bondurant Driving School at Sears Point that was now required before it was too late.

I have, from the original days of my father and his Pierce Arrows, occasionally driven like a racing car driver, at home behind the wheel of a responsive car, feeling at one with it, and making demands that respond to my touch. I don't mean in terms of speed—that always bored me—but how it handled the turns on a well-engineered mountain road without losing speed, while not burning rubber, and always staying on the correct side of the dividing line. So, it wasn't too different from a difficult and precise piece of surgery. It demanded my intense, unbroken concentration, yet without fatigue. In fact, where others drive tensely, I have always found driving relaxing and providing time to think about the issues ahead.

I checked in with Bob Bondurant and was accepted in spite of my age. I took the four days off from my practice, and in La Jolla Carol took the four days off from our mutual lives, not agreeing with my decision. Admittedly, this was the first time in my married life that I relied entirely on my own judgment in a decision that did affect our days together as a family. But it was now or never, and only I was at risk, life insurance being up to date. Carol was correct in her criticism of the fact that I could not insure the racing car, but I accepted this as a good reason to be careful and to rely on the expectation that such accidents were exceedingly rare with Bondurant. A wipeout of a new Datsun Z would cost $26,000. My concentration should therefore be enhanced by knowing this.

When the six of us signed in, we were taken by boss Bob Bondurant for a run in a van. He drove it like a race car, hitting the turns at high speed as we held our breaths. I never quite figured out what he meant to do, but I believe that the message was that if a van can do this, you had better expect more from a race car.

Then began our classes, one each day for at least two hours, where we had hammered into us the rules of the racing road, and what was expected of us in terms of safety. A bunch of little things, at least on the surface, in the end became big things. For the first two nights, my sleep was spasmodic as I went over the rules, concerned that my years might prove a limitation.

Now we were to go on the road. There were three of us and one instructor to a car, a small Datsun 4-door, and each of us took a turn at the wheel on the oiled surface designed to teach what a car does when you control its motion with hands and brakes, just as in the movie thrillers.

We would be told to make the move to spin the car by first touching the brakes sharply, quickly releasing, and at the same time whipping the wheel clockwise quickly as far as we could, and then letting go. The net result was that the car spun 180 degrees as it reached free fall. With hands off, it straightened out in the same driving line, though now backwards. How to get back in the original driving direction? Repeat the motions, and you are again heading home. My engineering lessons told me that this was all very logical, for the inertial energy was still directing the action, keeping us on line while we just danced in it. We had learned what all trained drivers know, and we did it.

The next two days were sheer joy as we drove Datsun Zs and Formula Ones full out. The great trick was  to touch the curb at the apex of the turn, marked by my teacher's foot, having braked a little to get there, and then gun out full blast as the turn is completed. On day two I got the devil from Steve, my coach, because I had not put up my hand as I made a pit-stop. He told me I wasn't concentrating. I disagreed, for as a surgeon, concentration was my most important trait. "I just slipped up," I said, and further stated that if I wasn't making it and was a danger to others and myself, he should wipe me out. Well, he didn't, for whatever reason.

On day three we had a time trial of which I was not aware, yet I managed to come in third out of the six. At least three were on their way to possible racing careers. One had just gotten second in that free-for-all race across the USA, having lost at the last minute when he didn't have chains. The winner did, as the racers hit the rare fall snowstorm at Donner Pass. The fourth was a broker from Boston, who kept his Porsche in the garage all winter, but how different the two of us were. He complained about his shoulders and arms aching during and after driving, something not happening to me, I guess, because this whole experience for me was a relaxation, with finger tip control of a fantastic machine.

So where was the joy? It was in the action of person and car on the high-speed turn, going full out and not burning rubber. When I would first get in the car and get all buckled in, I felt tense and concerned, perhaps afraid, as I tried to remember all of the regulations and precautions. Then I would grasp the wheel and hit the accelerator. The tenseness left immediately and it was one continuous "hurrah" from there on. I really didn't get any particular joy out of speeding full out on the straightaways. It was the cornering that was the challenge and my joy. I don't remember any speeds recorded, for our gauges only showed RPMs. I suppose that was a good idea.

Day three's highlight was the learning experience designed to test the limits of what a person and car can do when quick turns or sudden stopping are demanded. This was accomplished by a series of booths with traffic lights that at the last moment demanded quick brake or turn actions. The lessons were really directed at how, with speed, you have so little control, and made obvious the importance of distance between cars for safety. It also left me with a little more of a roving eye while driving, assessing the escape routes on the roadsides, should sudden swerves be required. Clearly, it is better to make these detours than try to stop, which puts you and the drivers, both in front and behind, also at risk.

This concern was already pretty well built in for me, for I remember so well an incident on the way to Carmel years before. I was driving a Mercedes sedan and noticed in my rear vision mirror an eighteen-wheeler going too fast over the bridge I had just crossed. It seemed likely that the driver did not know the road, for it suddenly became a narrow two-lane through the artichoke fields, and the workers were also known as notoriously bad drivers. In this instance, one had blocked the road. I stopped well away from the car ahead in order to have room to maneuver if required, for I could see smoke emerging from the truck's tires. He was not going to make the stop! I didn't wait to see if he could. I gunned my car off the road and into the artichoke field. The truck stopped just a few inches from the bumper of the car I had been behind. Someone was looking after me that day, though the eyes on the rear vision mirror get the credit. I hadn't yet been to Bondurant. I guess Dad trained his sons well.

On day four, we drove the small Formula cars, where one's buttocks almost scrape on the track itself. That day the big stock cars were warming up for the NASCAR race that weekend and were all around us, but we had the right of way on all occasions. I so well remember my bouncing rearview mirror being filled, from time to time, with the radiator and headlights of a big car as it stayed inches behind until I would raise my arm to let him pass on one of the short straightaways. He would go by with a hand signal and a broad smile. What fun!

One incident I will never forget. On day three, we were going all out, and the turn I loved most was a wide 180-degree turn that dipped and was so wonderfully banked that I drove on full acceleration throughout it. I broke out at the brow of the hill, full blast, to look down at another 180-degree turn, very tight, that would require a fair amount of braking. As I crested, I saw a strange sight—a car was parked at the apex of the turn facing directly towards me, as though monitoring our driving. My concentration did break as my subconscious said, "What a fool to be there in such danger." I felt my left front wheel catch slightly on the edge of the macadam. I sensed that I was in trouble, and that the car could be thrown off the road. Whether by luck, feel, or what I had learned on the oil, I braked and swung the wheel clockwise as far as I could to throw me into a spin, then released the wheel. The net result: I spun 180 degrees and I came to a stop parallel to the other car as though we were parked together. I looked at the other occupant, recognized him as Steve, my instructor, smiled, waved, and was off again at full speed. Did he wet his pants? I never asked him, but odds are he never again would pull that dumb stunt. My daily grade that had gone from a D to a C suddenly became a B for the last two days. We never spoke of our encounter, I am sure both feeling that lady luck had been our companion.

For me, the message was clear. At 65, I was still able to react to emergency danger in a positive fashion, and I don't remember getting the shakes later that I hear so much about. Yes, one learns something about oneself in unplanned, unforeseen ways, but it seemed that my joy in being part of a fine car at its top performance was the real thing and it was still in place. How fortunate can one be?

I drove home in my Cadillac Eldorado, enjoying its luxurious comfort and physical safety, without ever again feeling the desire to push the envelope.

CHAPTER

15.

From Berkeley to Napa

At home in the Napa Valley, commuting to Berkeley

By 1983, we had been living in the Napa Valley for thirteen years. We had moved from Berkeley after all of the girls were in college, for the city we loved had deteriorated. My proximity to Queen of the Valley Hospital in Napa, with a high-caliber staff, allowed me to fill a urological need there in my free hours, operating on many cases that were far from routine. Was I tempted to establish a new practice in this delightful wine country? No, for my pediatric practice in Oakland's Children's Hospital was a constant joy, and our caseload made possible more breakthroughs as the specialty continued to develop. Thus, I commuted for these thirteen years, forty-five miles each way, with plenty of time to think as I drove. Many times I would arrive home to have Carol tell me I must go back. My CB car radio wasn't effective, and cell phones were years away.

Although my fellow physicians in Berkeley had a hard time understanding how I could manage this commute of forty-five miles to and fro, they recognized that my "on call" availability had not changed. These years were as productive as ever.

Surgical scale creation—a last minute excursion

My passion about weight and water never ended as weighing patients before and after surgery became a hospital routine, but operative weight and water control was yet ahead. Dr. Edward Teller, creator of the hydrogen bomb, was on my TUR table for a prostatic resection, the risk of irrigant absorption and dilution of body cells, the brain included, always present. Why should this risk be tolerated? An operative scale could tell me minute-by-minute whether absorption was occurring. I would do something about it, in "Do it now" fashion, but I pondered how this might be achieved.

As I was nearing retirement, Terry Taylor, a new patient in his late sixties, was seen with a prostate suspicious to my finger, biopsies then proving the highest-grade prostatic carcinoma. I knew it would be fatal within a two-year span. We went for broke and started X-ray therapy, which proved disastrous, causing a degree of pain and urinary frequency unique in my experience. This remarkable man was made comfortable with a supra-pubic tube (catheter through the lower abdomen, rather than the urethra), which he changed himself, as he journeyed to and from Scandinavia. There, as well as in the Radiation Lab in Berkeley, he was a creative troubleshooting engineer in the radiological fields. Terry knew his prognosis and my helplessness. He asked if there was something he could create in the remaining time, for he could recognize my similar inquisitiveness. I said that a surgical scale could be a great contribution, badly needed as fluid imbalances in surgery were a major contributor to complications and even death. His dear friend David Moore, also a technical person in semi-retirement, was anxious to make a contribution. I was the passive member of the group, all of us with the same intention to contribute, financial returns not considered. We each contributed $15,000 eventually. I believe only Terry and I knew the disease with which we were dealing at the time. I knew full well he understood the situation.

We went to work in his living room, as he designed and built the scale, a massive and exact work of art. It was built by experts, from steel fabricator to cabinet maker. What resulted was a scale that we fixed firmly to the TUR table at the San  Francisco Veterans Hospital, where I was a consultant. The inert, supine patient could be continuously monitored throughout the procedure.

I was able to do twenty-five cases with the resident, demonstrating its sensitivity as we could recognize fluid overload while still correctable. I presented the paper at the AUA, expecting it to be immensely useful for the prostatic resection  (TURP), but also for the general surgeon operating for hours on the elderly, whose state of hydration was a critical component, yet only estimated with current methods. Overload with resulting cardiac failure was not rare. The operative scale also could prevent the fluid overload during endoscopic gynecological procedures. I gave it a try there, but no takers.

I play the patent game.

Gaining a patent for our surgical scale was another story. Our attorney was unable to get the necessary patent after three tries. To his chagrin, I asked if I could go to the Patent Office and make a direct presentation. I went to Washington and met a distinguished patent attorney, who took me to the Patent Office for my appointment with the examiner.

Each examiner is a young scientist, who spends ten consecutive years on the job while pursuing, fully paid, further education. My examiner was a tall, spare, studious man, who sat me down and said, "Tell me about it." I replied that I would have to educate him as to body physiology to make my points. He smiled and told me to go ahead. Over the next hour I took him through the whole process in my simplistic fashion. When I had finished, he said that I had made my points.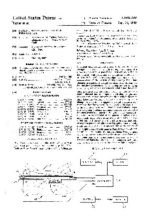

"But I haven't mentioned the scale."

"You don't have to. The need for the scale is obvious."

The patent was issued. I guess you would have to believe that this was really the last point in a process that assured success, but things didn't turn out that way. Terry Taylor, massive mind, passed away on almost the day I did our first case at the VA. At the least, he knew he had made another significant contribution. I think if we had gotten off the ground, the scale would eventually have been known as Taylor-Made.

To get off the ground was not to be, unbelievable as this might seem. From the moment of its appearance, resistance organized and was effective through silence. I was astounded to recognize that the bottleneck lay with the anaesthesia department. I was scheduled to present the scale to that group, but they made sure never to have the meeting. I ran a few cases myself, despite this resistance. The scale was a wonder. At a point every 10 minutes or so, when surgery lagged, I would say,"Hands off," and an accurate measurement was made. It was simply wonderful! Further, I found that body weight, and thus body water, that is kept normal throughout a procedure as IVs are monitored, allowed under-replacement of blood loss to be well tolerated.

So, I had to face the reality that Anaesthesia had enough on its plate. Not being humanists, they had no intention of upsetting their routines, no matter the price to the patient. Two articles on cerebral accidents appeared that presumed, without the slightest proof, to be from emboli (loose blood clots) at surgery, one in the *New England Journal of Medicine* (NEJM) and one in the *Journal of the American Medical Association* (JAMA). Diplomatically, I suggested that if someone would review pre- and post-operative body weights, fluid overload might be revealed as a more likely cause of cerebral edema acting like an embolus, but my notes remained unacknowledged. Our concept of advancing surgical care was thwarted.

How did we get from the experimental model, fixed to the TUR table, to the commercially-perfected lighter model I used in general surgery? I reached Scaletronics, the number one surgical scale maker, which had taken the lead away from Acme, the maker of my original

InBed Scale. David Hale, creative engineer and company founder, provided the final commercial scale. This is a beauty that is light and can be easily moved from table to table. It is accurate to 10 grams. It fits on both TUR and general surgery operating tables.  Without acceptance by anesthesiology, the scale lies gathering dust at the San Francisco VA hospital. I keep hoping that some unforeseen opportunity will arise that demands this added operative control, but it is not likely in my time. There is some positive fallout, for in the process, manufacturer David Hale took a next step when he constructed the first tiny scales for the newborn.

The surgical scale could have ranked with my original scale and leg wraps as a major contribution of which I could now be justly proud. As to effectiveness, I get a big zero. Had I known the outcome would I have gone ahead? Absolutely, not anticipating or even believing what would transpire. What is amazing is the combination of personalities, experience, training, and dedication that came together for this moment in time. I can only hope that his creativity and generosity to his last breath made Terry's passing more acceptable to him because he gave to the very end.

CHAPTER

16.

I Retire

Time to retire: at 67, it seemed the wise thing to do

The travel between Napa and Berkeley seemed to be lengthening as my professional responsibilities did not lessen. I now had two partners, yet I was still on duty many nights and weekends. Sixty-seven is a good time to call it quits, while physical and mental dexterity have not slipped. Giving up the pediatric work was the price I did not wish to pay. However, it seemed as if the specialty had made such advances in the realm of substituting less-invasive instrumentation that I would require special training better applied to the young urologists. I would be just treading water. Looking back, the decision was correct.

Does anyone know what retirement really means? I surely didn't, beyond expecting a little more time to improve my golf swing, read, cut the lawn, plant vegetables, and rove with my camera in the vineyards and wineries of the Napa Valley. Also, I could more actively support Carol as she sustained the Napa Valley Museum as President, envisioning a new museum and creating it. Using her artistic talents and enthusiasm, she would see this constructed on the expansive beautiful grounds of the Veterans Home in Yountville.

What then happened? "How to" books galore are written on retirement. They always suggest a list of possibilities. What they don't emphasize is that an active and fulfilling retirement requires years of getting ready for it, but how is this done? It demands enjoying your work, adding something to it each day, and then not accepting retirement as an escape. Retirement is a continuum, as curiosity, an open mind, and a "Do it now" habit finds new fields to explore, and the world is just sitting there waiting to be further explored. This is exactly what happened to me. No searching, just recognizing and doing it now, as has been habitual for me right along. Would I now tackle new problems? Yes and no, as my record of the next twenty years of a life in continuum is selective.

We had lived comfortably in a quiet Napa residential area with room for a vegetable garden and other joys of outside living. However, it was time for a change, and this took place just two years before retirement. Carol's artistic talents were given expression in a new home with a view on a hill not yet discovered by most. It was modeled after the work of architect Luis Barragán, whose homes in Mexico were striking for their lack of decoration, while their pastel walls, at times stark, radiated a kind of comfortable dignity that was Carol's style. We built our home and were alone on our hill for a little while, but within the year, dwellings below started to appear and hem us in. Then a serendipitous thing happened.

We move into a historic house

Lorrain and Judge Tom Kongsgaard had entertained us in their home on a bigger hill close by. Lorrain's mother had been living alone on the hill's crest until she passed away five years earlier. For some reason, this family mansion had remained off limits. We had wondered about it, but only as a curiosity. Then Lorrain suggested we see it sometime, it being reputed to be just an ugly concrete structure made from the concrete basalt building blocks her father had introduced to America. Its roof shingles were also concrete and fireproof, possibly the first such in the world.

I came home early one afternoon to find Carol in the kitchen. As she turned, I saw a strange look, her eyes hiding something.

I said, "Guess you either just made a killing at Lohmann's, or you looked at the house." (Lohmann's was a luxury clothes outlet in Concord).

"Well, I didn't go to Lohmann's, Dick."

My response was,"Then let's go look at the house."

We drove to the top of Stonecrest, walked around to the north side, and saw The View. It was so much like Dad's view of Mt. Diablo, when he built his house near Lafayette in the Hidden Valley he would later subdivide. Mt. St. Helena and the entire Napa Valley spread out before us as we stood next to the concrete block one-story house on a dry, grassy slope bounded by oaks to the south. For just a moment we stood in awe, then turned and got back in the car, as I said, "Next step is to have the girls see this." They did, and responded with a single judgment, "Dad, you're stuck." What they meant, I think, is that although we had been in our new home for only two years, now we would be on the move again.

Photography starts the ball rolling

Once settled in, after having turned the concrete bunker into a home, I found myself back in a photography mode, particularly as a storage closet became a darkroom. This was a day when the films were just black and white or Kodachrome, a far cry from today's digital world. I was ready to go back into action, for a darkroom had not been available for 15 years. With my Leica, Pentax, and Nikkormat cameras in hand, I roved the valley, believing that both black-and-white and color would be needed to capture what I might see.

With the sudden loss of the exhilaration of my pediatrics work, I found myself with camera in hand, wandering though vineyards and wineries, just looking to see what was there. My Pentax with black-and-white 400 Tri-X film would get a workout.

It had been a long time since I had worked in my spacious, wonderful dark room in Berkeley, so what to do about this? Our new house had a 10x6 foot closet just outside the kitchen with bare floor, walls, and ceiling and no running water. This would have to do, and I adjusted by trucking my water in and out in pails. I carefully placed used solutions in multiple bottles, because I couldn't take the chance of damaging our vineyard with septic tank effluent containing photographic chemicals.

Jimo Perini, photo mentor

Another mentor appeared at the right time. Kathy was to be married at home on our spacious lawn backed by the Chardonnay vineyard. She had just met Jimo Perini, possibly the most accomplished 35 mm. black-and-white photographer in the world. In a weak moment, he had agreed to photograph her wedding, just minutes before flying into the stratosphere on his next assignment abroad. We became instant friends, and he became my mentor in tricks of the trade that would spur me on as I recorded what my roving eye would discover in our beautiful valley.

Vineyard forays were incessant. I would often stop the car and climb over a fence to talk to the boss or the owner of a vineyard. I was sold on my new world, typified by the elderly grower who, when asked what he would do if his tractor broke down in the midst of a busy season, answered, "I would go next door to my neighbor." But then he added, "It is not quite that simple, because I have three neighbors and I run the risk of hurting the feelings of the other two." What a delightful world, and it hasn't ever changed.

We become growers and wine makers

An inside look at the wine world was at our front door. John Kongsgaard, son of our neighbor, wine maker and viticulturist combined, had planted grapes on our half acre to the east. The judge had an acre of Chardonnay, his and ours, and a few rows of  choice Zinfandel grapes that would be processed by the Judge and his friends. Two hundred cases was the goal easily achieved each year.

We had been in our hilltop home for just a year when Tom and Lorrain made a trip abroad. As he left, Tom said, "You're in charge."

"In charge of what?"

"The pick, of course."

I was on the hook, a neophyte, but such challenges were not new. I enlisted Tom's daughter, Mary, and with the help of neighbors and John's field worker team to do the picking, we had the wine "cooking" in the barrels on the Judge's return. His surprise and relief was obvious. To me, the implications were otherwise. I had been projected into a new world. I was hooked, and would run with it.

The next several years were devoted to just another search to understand the process, this time not looking for a solution. Process was quite enough. I had a living library from which to learn, as founders in their seventies and eighties never had lost their joy in the vineyards and their desire to pass on what they had learned to anyone interested enough to ask the questions. This had always been natural for me. It led to long sessions with the tape recording in the background, their voices now preserved for posterity in our Valley Wine Library in St. Helena. I absorbed their wisdom to the point that my "dumb" questions had no answers, as I probed the borders of their art. My camera also was working, and black-and-white portraits are on the library wall. They will stay black, not become brown with time, for as was always my habit in practice when exploring a new way to do something, immediate success had to result in long term success, for a lifetime is so short. A new batch of hypo fixing solution was made for each portrait. Who are these immortals? Nathan Fay, Charles Wagner, Roy Raymond, Joseph Heitz, Maynard Amarine, Andre Tchelistcheff, Louis Martini, Brother Timothy, and Robert Mondavi, all now gone, while Joseph Phelps, Warren Winiarsky, Robert Travers, Peter Mondavi, Joseph Grgich, and Angelo Regusci are still on the job. "Doing it now" with my camera has paid off in spades.

As the process became clearer, my camera whirred, often now using movie film. My questions mounted as they raised more questions, always answered, until I, embarrassed at my invasion, waved goodbye. This was the "chosen land" that had chosen Carol and me to enter.

I am now a publisher

The next logical step was for me to become a book creator and then a publisher. How could that be? It is always just such a dream for so many. Carol was responsible. She had repeatedly said, "Dick you have learned so much from these men and taken so many pictures of what they do, shouldn't you write a book providing the fundamentals buried in the texts?" It had never occurred to me, but now it seemed an obligation, for so many desired to know, as Bob Mondavi was exposing the wonders of wine to the world.

How would I make it go? The businessman that Dad trained now expressed himself. The book would have to be black and white at first to make it possible financially. I stumbled on Moshe Shor, a man of immense integrity, who could do the printing in Korea. With help from a graphic artist, Judy, the job was done. I made a "dummy" and named it *Vine to Wine*. I took the dummy to Silverado Country Club, to the principal bank in town, and to Saylor and Hill, my brother-in-law's insurance firm in Oakland. All three organizations had more than just a taste for wine. With the bargain price a little above cost, they all agreed to invest in my project. The income from 3,500 books paid publishing expenses, leaving $1,500 for profit. It would be a dollar spent for a dollar earned, and Dad would be happy.

Vine to Wine I was so successful that another 10,000 copies found their way abroad and into our valley, as I, now the salesman, pushed my books in every kind of outlet from winery tasting rooms to drug stores. It was just plain fun, for as Dad had taught me, 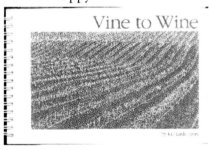 "Dick, if you believe in what you are selling, even an Eskimo will buy your refrigerator."

I was also sensitive to the growing appeal of color in publications. So, for four years I compiled a journal or daybook, telling the story of vineyard and winery in color in a day-to-day fashion. All of these were intended to teach those who wished to know. Three thousand journals were lapped up each year. At the same time, I had the joy of learning more each day, my camera solidifying every memory. I was welcomed in all of the wineries, tasting rooms, and work areas, and was even able to photograph the night picking just beginning in the Carneros region. My literary adventures were nothing more than an expression of the Process Mind trying to understand, and in this way remember.

Vine to Wine II *is created and I become a better salesman.*

With an immense store of wine-related Kodachromes, it was logical to create *Vine to Wine II* in color and hard cover. This, too, was well received; some 15,000 copies sold across America. It now resides on Amazon and is likely to become a classic, as no one has appeared to repeat my desire to teach, and not just to impress. At the least, it will remain a primer that tells how things were back when.

A National Geographic photographer, already famous for his recent work here in our valley, turned to me at lunch one day and said, "Dick, how do you take your pictures?"

My answer was "Are you kidding me? I won't carry coal to Newcastle."

He answered, "No, I mean it."

My response was, "OK. I am driving, often on an errand, and my eye sees something special. I stop the car, and get out, trying not to be hit by a passing car, and then over the fence I go. I walk up to a worker, show him my camera, and ask, 'May I please take a picture of what you are doing?' He rarely understands my words, but we communicate somehow. With a broad smile he says 'Si.' That's it."

"Thanks Dick, I guess I have a ways to go. Perhaps my whitening hair will help, for when I do just what you did, I am perceived as an agent of the Immigration Service and backs are turned." Once again, as I have always believed as I take photos, "it's all in the eyes" of the photographer and the photographed alike.

Wildflowers seen by my macro lens

The years went by but nothing changed for me, then in my eighties. I was blessed with fine health. My golf swing became shorter and shorter, the compensation being that I hit the ball straighter and straighter, but the fun with the "big hit," no matter its course, was gone. So what? If the old head would stay active, how could I ask for anything more?

Well, there was more. This continues to be the saga of a guy who, as he walks, looks down, kicks pebbles aside, and uncovers precious Indian arrowheads, unnoticed for years, that open up a new vista to be studied. This was the case with wildflowers.

I had driven hundreds of miles in my forays into vineyards, wineries, and bookstores, eyes always on the road. But these wide-open-orbs discovered beauty everywhere, as peripheral vision kept noticing splotches of color on the roadsides. These were wildflowers. They took me back to Boy Scout days, when I had searched for magnificent Trillium, determined it would be the prize among my required fifty flowers for a wildflower merit badge.

Over many years this desire to recognize the varieties surfaced many times, but I was always frustrated by the published texts that covered too many flowers in too many places, and not always in full color. I had all the books from basic *Peterson* on up, but even he, either running out of money or wishing for more profit, depicted most of the flowers as plain line drawings and left me uninformed.

The Problem: too many pictures with too little identifying information to find specimens. The Solution: take photos as I drove, trying to stay safe from passing cars, then at home study and identify them. I would stick to what was familiar here in the Napa Valley. The photos did it, for I was doubly blessed with my Nikkormat, purchased so long ago. It has a very special macro lens, equally good for landscapes. I could photograph from infinity to as close as two inches. I chose to shoot at two feet, and thus mimic what the eye would see comfortably, not tempted to take extreme close-ups that are dramatic only as works of art.

Once again, something unexpected happened: The photos and their descriptions became another book, as I tried to apply my yearning to know and make it possible for others to share my joy in knowing.

100 Napa County Roadside Wildflowers

The books would appear in bookstores and hotels as I varied my rounds to contact likely outlets, for I no longer had the luxury of the built-in customers to whom wine had an appeal. To make sure of my data, I enlisted Jake Ruygt, prominent horticulturist, to verify the flowers and amplify the descriptions. On my Apple computer I assembled all and made ready for publication. This was delayed for five months as I waited for Jake's contributions. I finally laid down the law, because precious time was being lost as a season was racing by. Jake's rejoinder was, "But Dick, you have so much energy!" I responded, "Jake, don't you know the difference between energy and enthusiasm?" His needed insights were on my desk in a week. The job was done.

Two printings of 3,000 each met local demands, as this handy little handbook, sturdy and small enough for a back pocket or purse, saturated the market. It remains today the local bible for adults and children alike. My quick-memory limitations force me from time to time to refer back to my own book, always available in the car as we drive the winding roads ringing our valley and look for the appearance of each flower at its appointed time. The 100 are always there, although locations shift. For instance, wild marigolds are invading and pushing aside long-dominant mustard, orange for yellow, making each day a time to see something new.

Today, my digital Nikon clicks away so easily and cheaply that it makes a photographer out of anyone. I refuse to fall into that trap. Every photo must tell a story. On my computer, I will only sharpen an image, or perhaps make the shading more real, as under- and over-exposures inevitably crop up. Now, on my Apple, I can make a DVD, either with motion or still photos. I favor the latter, for I am allowed time to contemplate.

The computer discovers me, and I take the plunge into the new world

This brings me to the part the computer has played and is playing in my life, as the physical limitations of age impinge on my ability to climb fences and stoop in wineries to catch the bubbles of fermentation. So, I make do and recall and learn.

On retirement, I made it a point to spend time with Frank Hinman Jr. in his permanent office, the privilege of UC's retired professors. Frank would be at his computer. At first, I couldn't understand his enthusiasm for this new gimmick, but he won, and I purchased the Leading Edge, a clone of the pioneering IBM. I was off, and walking, yet tiptoeing. Like most older people, I feared I would fail to make it work. I didn't know then of the relationship of simple algebra that I loved to the mechanics of putting data together that the computer made possible. Fear abated almost immediately as I probed the computer mind. We were simpatico. It knew what it was doing; I would find out what it was doing. It just required patience, and trial and error. The *something* I might be looking for was always there, somewhere.

Frank was an Apple computer user from the start. I joined him with my Apple Performa, as I recognized its ability with graphics. I could illustrate and back up a photo message with words. Both color books were created on my Apple, then transferred to a disc and sent to Korea, where the finest of printers electronically did the rest. Could I have composed this story without its help? Not a chance, but there is much more.

I discover the Web

About 12 years ago, I signed on to a chat group of pediatric urologists centered in Chicago at high-level academia. There is little doubt that I am the oldest correspondent by at least twenty years, and I try to conduct myself accordingly. This means taking a truly diplomatic approach to each problem, my comments based on both principle and experience that no one else can have at his fingertips, coupled with patience on my part. I have always allowed the others to first have their say. I speak up not in criticism but only if I have something positive to add. They, in turn, keep me posted on the challenges they face, so that I can keep up with what is new.

Have I been effective? At times, I believe so, and that is reward enough. It is the rare person whom I will never meet, save on the Web, who I hope feels encouraged to follow the basic principles I present as taught me by the best of mentors.

If there is immensely productive and satisfying fallout, it is abroad, where the luxury of the so-called pediatric urologist often is not possible. In deprived lands, the pediatric surgeon at times must be a urologist as well. There, the child may be considered a burden, often close to starvation, and is denied care in the general urologist's and physician's offices. If lucky, these children end up in the hands of a pediatric surgeon who must embrace a discipline for which he or she is not trained.

The Web brings pediatric urology to Pakistan

Ten years ago, a Web correspondent from the city of Gujranwala, Pakistan (population 4 to 5 million), asked the chat group devoted to pediatric urology for help as he faced urological problems for which he had not been trained. Irfan Mirza is a pediatric surgeon, and an Assistant Professor at the University in Lahore. He was finding that these credentials and abilities were not enough to meet his needs, for children arriving at his door often had serious congenital deformities of the unfamiliar genitourinary system. He would not turn them away. He believed he must also become competent in this new field and asked for help, for the possibility of gaining academic training remained nonexistent as he answered the daily calls.

I followed my rule of waiting for responses from my young peers before speaking up. When three weeks' time brought none, I emailed Dr. Irfan Mirza directly, outside the pediatric urological group, offering my help. Thus began a decade of mentoring, which benefited me as much as I hope it has Irfan. His handling of his first case of a UPJO (blocked kidney), made obvious that I was dealing with a Process Mind. My ordered approach to diagnosis and treatment should be readily understood. I was thrilled to again be effective.

With what did he have to work? The basic "8 steps" could be followed, and Irfan's X-ray equipment allowed a prompt and inexpensive intravenous pyelogram, the IVP (that reveals kidney function and anatomy). This was an immense plus, for in America the expensive and cumbersome CT scan and MRI had become the rule, pushing aside the most valuable urological tool of all, the IVP. I was thrilled to be thus limited, for the IVP is still the queen of studies, relegating the also new, inexact, ultrasound to a backup position.

Irfan has become a competent endoscopist, able to define bladder and urethra characteristics and orifice configurations, as he is so often faced with damaging ureteral reflux. With standard kidney function measurements, Irfan and I were in a position to together practice top-caliber medicine, and his abilities as an artist made his surgical descriptions live for me.

He quickly learned to pass X-rays directly to me on the Web using Eastman's free OFOTO. The films are as clear as if made here. Irfan was at home with the computer. On more than one occasion, I checked my Apple every hour, day and night, as he struggled to save a young life. My experience with fluid electrolyte balance several times made the difference, as he grasped the fine points, particularly as to the need for potassium in a humid country plagued with diarrheas. Were little lives saved as he too stayed up all night? The answer is a simple yes, as Irfan learned the importance of body weight, the urine density, and specific replacement needs. I was back to having my idea of fun again, although in my eighties and nineties. We now consult less often, for he has learned the ropes, and yet, when a tough case comes along, the communication flies, thanks to the World Wide Web.

Irfan is fifty three, with a wife and two grown daughters, one studying architecture in the university, and the other having just finished her surgical residency at the University in Lahore. He has been a teacher of anatomy as a demonstrator, and is an Assistant Professor of Pediatric Surgery in Lahore. As a pediatric surgeon in private practice,  he serves a populace in the millions. His hospital, supported by the Rafig Anwar Memorial Hospital Trust, gives him a staff and his own operating room. He drives 100 kilometers to medical school in Lahore six times a week. I think the exactness of our science is a joy for his Process Mind, for, as a urologist and not only a pediatric surgeon, he no longer needs to *explore* for a diagnosis, which is so often the case with childhood anomalies involving heart, lungs, and abdomen, and even the head. What have we accomplished this far? Irfan Mirza is easily one of the best-trained "residents" I have ever had—among the top six out of hundreds. I smile as I describe this as a teacher-student relationship, for this "student" is known throughout his country for the humanitarian and scientific responsibilities he carries as a leader. Much of our correspondence is direct, bypassing the confusing information practiced by our experts. Irfan understands this and is now wedded to the Hinman-Schulte-Lyon basics, and with consistent success, has seen little reason to listen to the varying points of view on the Web.

Beyond this, the variety and number of serious cases in Pakistan is ten times ours. If there is any frustration on my part, it is because others here have not recognized their obligations abroad, and do not share my joy in being wonderfully useful. A good example is the number of cases of boys with Posterior Urethral Valve (PUV) that he and others in Pakistan and India see in a single year—probably ten times our numbers—and we haven't the vision to see what we could do to take advantage of this learning potential, while at the same time providing succor.

The majority of PUVs in Pakistan are not seen until kidney damage is great. Urinary diversion by ureterostomy is their only hope to survive long enough to allow the dialysis and kidney transplantation processes to develop in that world. Constant kidney drainage requires western collection devices, but their use there is limited by ignorance and poverty.

So, what to do? Irfan and I are struggling with this at the moment, but there is so far to go. We Americans, so often isolated from reality, deprive ourselves of this opportunity to accomplish what freedom makes possible.

I will continue to work abroad with pediatric surgeons in India, Romania, Brazil, Mexico, and other countries which, fortunately, are still aware of the value of the basics that are available to them, intending to practice urology at the highest level.

Time makes my inquiring mind wonder how the episodes just recounted could have occurred in a single lifetime. My mind pushes night and day, seeming to be as inquisitive as ever, while muscles and bones struggle to keep up.

CHAPTER

17.

I Try to Discover How It All Happened

The Process Mind in retrospect

As we drove from Sonoma to Napa one day, daughter Laura said, "Dad, I think you should write today what your thoughts are as to how our minds work." So, here it is, as I relate my experiences with the hope that a few young people may gain insight as to how they think, as they seem to struggle with their identities. It will require some repetition, but here goes.

My first manifestation of the Process Mind came when I tinkered, taking things apart to see what made them tick (and not always able to get them back together without having some nuts and bolts left over). My asking, and then searching for "Why?" was on its way.

My next encounter would seem to have been when I was encouraged to get all A's in school, and somehow I didn't think this important. I had noticed that my friends with all A's always received A's. So I guessed the teachers were biased and, if so, I would not receive the benefit of the doubt, for I was slower to learn as my memory, so dependent on understanding, took second place to the Quick Memories of my best friends.

There was something else in play, however. I loved the logic of Algebra that always seemed to start with something as simple as 2 x 2 = 4. I feared the memorization demanded in trigonometry, where formulas were the rule and therefore must be accepted at face value and memorized to be available for testing. This showed up strikingly when I came close to failing Descriptive Geometry in my first Stanford semester. It was really an advanced Trigonometry. I dropped out of Engineering, convinced that I was just too dumb to make it.

Dr. Bacon, Professor of Mathematics, thought otherwise. His intervention put me back on course. It was then, for some assurance, that I gained Mom's admission that my Terman IQ score was 136, and there was hope. I was thankful not to be in the gifted category, where varied talents so often lead to a confusion in goals, not my style where just making the most of each day was quite enough. With a sigh of relief, I accepted that I would have to just study longer and harder. With persistence, I could get there, whatever or wherever "there" might be.

The next example of the Process Mind in action came when Dr. Hedburg, professor of Engineering Hydraulics, gave me the highest grade in the class, as I *developed* the formulas others took for granted and applied.

Up to this point, the direction of my life was not different from that of carpenters, electricians, mechanics, and plumbers who, with common sense and process-driven minds daily figure out a better way to do things. When I ask them if they can memorize easily, or are they good spellers, they just laugh, often volunteering that, "I wouldn't be here if I could memorize and spell and get the grades to be a real professional."

"You mean straight A's?"

"Of course."

I have often asked myself, "Could I have gotten into medical school without the help of those in power who knew me well?" It's unlikely, and today, with thousands of applicants, the personal interview as a decision-maker is rarely possible. Yet, medical advances suffer as the person who asked the dumb questions is likely to be excluded.

The improvements in medical care that I developed would seem to serve as examples of the Process Mind in action. Here are two of them.

1. In 1948, the recognition was just waiting to be made that slow

venous flow could play a major part in the embolus formation leading to dislodgment and death. It had been overlooked for years. Why? A Process Mind had not been challenged, I suspect. The Quick Memory minds of immensely competent physician researchers believed that improved anticoagulation was the only way to go.

Time and place now get into the act. Not only was the Process Mind to be challenged, but the problem, always there, had to be recognized. Further, that Process Mind had to be prepared, as was I, by Bernoulli's fluid-flow theorem that played a major part in my "A" at Stanford. Was this a special time? I think not, for the anticoagulant Heparin had been in use for years. It was the place that counted. I was there, saw the need, and acted. I "did it now." All that remained to do was to be effective, the keystone of any advance.

2. The intrusion into fluid electrolyte balance also required the Process Mind, with time and place making the final difference. The Feldman fluid overload was accepted by medical experts, as "The Book" was followed. A Process Mind had to be walking through the ward that very day and be stopped in his tracks by the sight. Ingrained curiosity took over: the Process Mind saw Mr. Feldman as a problem to be solved. It appeared that liver failure met all of the criteria for that diagnosis, but the Process Mind demanded to go one step further. Symptoms are the end-points of a problem. Thus, I had to search out and define the problem itself before instituting treatment.

The "eight steps" of Dr. Frank Hinman is a natural outcome of the Process Mind that demands understanding before a diagnosis is made. When the eight steps are taken, then a consistent diagnosis will be the result, time and time again.

I had difficulty in mastering a foreign language, something my Quick Memory friends found not a problem. While cycling through Germany, conversation in the shops enabled Ted and me to build a working colloquial vocabulary of about 800 words, so happy were the people to help. However, on returning to college, my two years of Scientific German led nowhere, for when I attempted to translate German, it was a total loss because of its grammar that places the verb always at the end of each sentence, no matter how wordy.

On the other hand, I loved my two grammar school years of Latin that still provide insight into our own language. Was this the Process Mind expressing itself as language foundation roots were exposed? I think so.

With music, leaving pure talent aside (an obvious personal loss), many hours at the keyboard were necessary for me just to play from memory a tune or two. My lack of a Quick Memory seems the likely culprit, and again hard work and persistence were the only ways of making up the difference. An absence of talent made this untenable.

Perhaps this discussion is too detailed. However, it is my attempt to make the encouragement of the Process Mind not only the responsibility of one's self, but also that of parents and teachers, and ultimately medical schools. The latter still lag behind many law schools and most business schools, who actively search for curious, prepared Process Minds as leaders for the future. The medical school counters with the new major of Biomechanics. This will prove no substitute for the same creative Process Minds with disciplines in Engineering and Physics, then fine-tuned by the third dimension of patient care, which only medical school and residencies can provide. It is the hands on of the physician, combined with the process itself, that makes for discovery. An allowance of ten percent in each class for engineers wishing to be doctors would, by having the "dumb" questions asked, encourage the Quick Memories to light up their Process Mind qualities, and all would prosper.

These are all afterthoughts of one given the privilege of extra years and bequeathed the health to enjoy them.

<h1 align="center">Epilogue</h1>

Final foray ? Perhaps not

The Process Mind is never quiet. I have a problem, now well defined, and it must be solved if I can safely continue driving in ever busier traffic. The apparent problem is that I am 93. The real problem is that my elderly neck is stiffening, and I find looking back before a lane-change takes too long as I take my eyes from the road ahead, which increases the danger of a rear-end collision. The stress of driving is increased, for even in younger years the need to look back before a lane change has always been accompanied by apprehension.

My acceptance that nothing was being done to correct this need didn't hit home until six years ago. I recalled that my much-loved twenty-six-year-old niece, Lee Lyon, had been trampled to death by a charging elephant being freed from captivity to the wilds. Lee was an accomplished wildlife photographer. Something went wrong. Only if her camera was mistakenly on "wide angle"—as the warning on my right convex car mirror warns that "Objects in the mirror are closer than

they appear"—could this tragedy have taken place. The Process Mind went into action, the solution sought in characteristic "Do it now" fashion.

As with my approach to medical diagnosis, facts must first be

183

assembled. These were:

1. The convex mirror on the right does away with the blind spot, but it does not accurately identify the position or speed of a car that is approaching or is in it.

2. The State Highway Patrol states that two to three car lengths of separation makes for a safe lane change. I chose to accept three car lengths, roughly fifty feet, as the desirable distance.

Solution: In our spacious driveway, Carol's Jeep was placed 50 feet behind my vehicle. Its image on my right-side convex mirror was 2" x 2". A prototype 2" x 3" Target/Frame, cut from a picnic plate and attached to the mirror, enclosed this image as the car moved from a greater distance to the 50-foot mark. I tested it on the road. The Target/Frame worked. As long as the following car's image remained within the frame and not moving through it, a safe lane change was assured. I had only to quickly glance, without a head turn, keeping my eyes on the road ahead. The surprise was the accuracy of recognizing the speed of an overtaking car as it moved against the frame, now as a reference point.

The left driver's side mirror presented a different problem. It is flat and its narrower field of vision, no matter how accurately it is placed, cannot fully eliminate a blind spot. The suitable Target/Frame, larger than on the right convex mirror (closer eye-to-mirror distance) also revealed a closing speed, yet my apprehension as I changed lanes still remained. I could not trust that the blind spot had been fully eliminated.

It was logical, then, to duplicate the right-side mirror of the same convexity, applying it to the flat left mirror, leaving enough flat mirror area in place to comply with the law. The many small mirrors now available come nowhere close to my demands, for their hyperconvexities reveal tiny images that defy judgment as to position and speed. They serve only as warnings that something is there.

My patent request for the Target/Frame was prepared and denied. Why? Because an almost identical patent, drawings and all, had been issued in 1999, yet was not in effect because of nonpayment of maintenance fees. Thus, I can freely make this long-term solution to a driving hazard that accounts for 500,000 accidents each year! The automobile industry has kept its doors locked against any intrusion into its electronic trials with radar. However, the recent Toyota experience is perhaps a warning that complex electromagnetic systems may carry risks.

To try to be effective, I am placing this solution in the public's domain through Google and You Tube. The only hindrance is habit, and I find it formidable. However, as years become minutes in my time, my habit of identifying problems, then solving them, and finally, being effective serves me well. I now drive without stress, with just glances instead of head turns, my eyes never leaving the road ahead.

Dr. William Parry, Emeritus Professor of Urology at the University of Oklahoma, has his rigid neck in a brace as he drives thousands of miles a year to meet his responsibilities. Only with his bilateral convex mirrors and Target/Frames is this possible.

My Process Mind keeps churning, and it says over and over again:

Recognize and unearth the Real Problem

Fix it

Do It Now

Be Effective